Tastefully Small

Finger Sandwiches

EASY PARTY SANDWICHES FOR ALL OCCASIONS

BY KIM HENDRICKSON

ISBN-13: 978-0-9844315-2-6

Library of Congress Cataloging-in-Publication Data
Hendrickson, Kim, 1954–
   Finger sandwiches : easy party sandwiches for all occasions / by Kim Hendrickson.
      p. cm. -- (Tastefully small)
   Includes bibliographical references and index.
   ISBN-13: 978-1-60138-266-5 (alk. paper)
   ISBN-10: 1-60138-266-9 (alk. paper)
   1. Appetizers. I. Title.
   TX740.H4674 2008
   641.8´12--dc22   2008015655
                          10 9 8 7 6 5 4 3

COVER DESIGN: Catherine Rawson and Brett Rand Guldemond (Rand & Rawson Studios)
PHOTOGRAPHY: Tricia Solyn
ILLUSTRATIONS: Leslie Kruzicki
INTERIOR DESIGN: Meg Buchner

Printed in China

For my father, the wonderful human being he was.

menues parceles ensemble sunt beles

small packages considered together are beautiful

13th-century French expression

Sandwich Bouquet, page 84.

Acknowledgements

Some say it takes a village to raise a child. In my case it took a very large group of friends to bring this book to completion. I only hope that those I've neglected to mention below know what an important role they have played in the process of creating this book and series. I want to thank:

Doug Brown, for his support and kindness throughout the years and his willingness to see me published; Linda Kosarin, for kick-starting the creative process by creating the beautiful cover of this book; Tricia Solyn, for her unflagging enthusiasm and patience when taking even the most frustrating photos; Leslie Kruzicki, who came in at the final hour to fill this book with lovely instructional watercolors; Bari Gilbert, for her unending variety of initial interior designs and diagrams; Diane Cossin, Patty Logan and Mary Ellen Legge, whose "red pens" did overtime correcting and proofing these recipes; my friends John Rutledge, Sam Testa, Kat Lau, Eric Dow, and David Burke for their never-ending support of me in all of my creative endeavors; Dean Karrel and George Stanley at John Wiley for their continued interest and encouragement; and finally, Alan Muskat, for his keen eye in all aspects of this book, from detailed editing and photo correction to stellar flap and backcover text, savvy marketing and promotion advice, and for never permitting me to think that I could not accomplish anything I put my energies toward. I am forever grateful for his help and inspiration.

Table of Contents

Foreword

Introduction

Knife-Cut Sandwiches

Smoked Turkey and Dried Fruit Pâté Squares...................14
Cucumber and Shrimp Triangles 16
Curry Cashew Bites...18
Caper and Green Tea Squares...20

Cutter-Shaped Sandwiches

Cucumber Apricot Flowers 24
Smoked Salmon Hearts 26
Fiesta Chicken Squares..28
Confetti Spread Butterflies...30
Bacon Chutney Tulips 32
Tea-Smoked Egg Diamonds 34

Open-Faced Sandwiches

Beef, Apple, and Watercress Spirals 38
Austrian Cheese Triangles...40

Mock Crab Flowers...42

English Style Potted Ham Shapes 44

Stilton Pear Bites 46

Rolled, Stacked, and Carved Sandwiches

Avocado Pine Nut Layers..50

Olive Spread Pinwheels 52

Hummus Stacks..54

Herbed Cheese Gift Boxes 56

Tomato-Eyed Pyramids..58

Tarragon Egg Boxes 60

Pressed and Shaped Sandwiches

Caviar-Tipped Rolls..64

Grape, Brie, and Walnut Cups.....................................66

Peach Scallop and Ceviche Tulips..............................68

Jamaican Beef Turnovers 70

Sweet Sandwiches

Lime Curd Boxes 74

Jam 'n Sponge Crosses...76

Asian Pear Harvest Sandwiches 78

Banana Morsels..80

Plated Sandwich Ideas

Sandwich Bouquet...84

Dotted Roast Beef Sandwich Plate 86

Stained Glass Sandwiches.....................................88
Sandwich Stacks 90

Scoops

Stuffed Tomato Cups..94
Italian Shrimp and Beans 96
Lentil Duck-Filled Grapes....................................98
Danielle's Veggie Platter....................................100

Kid-Friendly Sandwiches

Pineapple Cheese Flowers 104
Nutty Carrot Rounds 105
Apple Yogurt Happy Faces.....................................106

What to Do with Leftover Bread?

Bread Crumbs 110
Croutons 111
Savory Mushroom Bread Pudding................................112
Tomato Spinach Strata..114

Appendix

Blanching Vegetables 117
Toasting Nuts 118

Resources   119

Index 121

Foreword

Having owned a tea room for fourteen years, I know how much handwork goes into the creation of beautiful finger sandwiches. I also know the delight that comes to the eyes of guests as they behold these delicate morsels of delicious whimsy. I have seen entire tables of diners "ooh" and "ahh" at the presentation of a three-tier silver tray bearing fantastic pinwheels, triangles, squares and swirls, all designed to amuse the spirit as well as the appetite. "Too beautiful to eat" has to be the most uttered phrase in the modern British or American tearoom.

Having tasted these works of art, finger sandwich enthusiasts are no longer content to simply consume two slices of bread with a common spread or meat. Their appetites are only appeased when all their senses are pleased.

Kim Hendrickson has brought new respect to the art of finger sandwiches. This collection of tiny delectables is sure to be a staple in the kitchens of both professional and once-in-a-while chefs. Whether you are preparing a beautiful afternoon tea, an informal reception, a wedding shower, or a simple children's birthday party, Kim has designed the perfect savory showpiece that will satisfy any appetite and make you look as though you have been catering events all your life. How tasteful is that?

Bruce Richardson, author of *The Great Tea Rooms of Britain, Tea in the City,* and *The New Tea Companion*

Introduction

When I think of finger sandwiches, I think of my grandmother having tea with her lady friends. The image of them daintily lifting the squishy white bread with their red-lacquered fingernails, in between puffs of Pall Mall cigarettes, is etched in my memory. When I was small, I wanted to be a lady, just like my grandmother!

Fortunately, times have changed. I've grown up, never smoked, and don't paint my nails, but I do still long for those little sandwiches.

Today, sandwiches are a fashion statement. If you are not eating a grilled panini or an overstuffed wrap, you aren't eating a sandwich! I crave the great flavors of today in yesterday's delicate sandwich presentation. Variety, artful craftsmanship, delicious ingredients, and small size are the principles that inspired me to write this book.

Truth is, aesthetics do matter. Whether one is choosing a cookie from an assorted platter or a savory from a deli showcase, we always gravitate to the most attractive one. The same is true for sandwiches. Offer great flavor in an attractive and unique format and you will have a successful party and happy guests.

In this book, you'll find a whole spectrum of stylish and sumptuous sandwiches starting with the simplest of presentations and culminating in elaborate "works of art." Sandwich shapes and styles can also be interchanged with most fillings, giving you a multitude of choices for your next hors d'oeuvre party, casual gathering, or afternoon tea. Most recipes can be easily converted to standard-size lunch sandwiches as well if you choose.

Small is beautiful, yesterday and today. When tasty and attractive is the goal and easy is a must, one or more of these straightforward recipes will surely fill the bill.

Enjoy every tasteful bite.

Clockwise from left: Confetti Spread Butterflies, page 30; Hummus Stacks, page 54; Cucumber and Shrimp Triangles, page 16.

Knife-Cut Sandwiches

These sandwiches are the simplest to prepare. But as long as your fillings are delicious, no one will notice. Garnished edges add class to any basic sandwich.

- Smoked Turkey and Dried Fruit Pâté Squares
- Cucumber and Shrimp Triangles
- Curry Cashew
- Caper and Green Tea

Smoked Turkey & Dried Fruit Pâté Squares

The summer memory of really good, light chicken salad with seasonal fresh fruit within it lingers on my taste buds. This winter version of that salad is an easy, sweeter reproduction.

Yield: 24 sandwiches

½ cup dried figs

½ cup dried peaches or dried apricots

¼ cup dried cranberries

¼ cup almonds, toasted

1 cup smoked turkey breast

3 green onions, sliced
  (use both white and light green parts)

¼ cup cream cheese, softened

¼ cup sour cream

2 tablespoons honey

⅛ teaspoon ground allspice

6 slices pumpernickel bread

6 slices rye or wheat bread

Using a food processor, chop the figs, peaches, cranberries, and almonds into small pieces with a few short pulses, then remove mixture and set aside. Chop turkey and green onions briefly with quick pulses of the food processor; add cream cheese, sour cream, honey, and allspice, using just a few more pulses to combine the ingredients.

Add the fruit and nuts; pulse once or twice just to combine. Be careful not to overchop. Place mixture in a bowl, cover, and refrigerate until ready to use.

Spread the filling equally on rye or wheat slices, then top with the pumpernickel slices to create 6 sandwiches. Using a serrated knife, remove crusts and cut into 4 equal, square sandwiches.

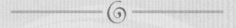

Little Bits

Create some contrast. Take advantage of the wide variety of breads available for both their color and texture. An all-white sandwich is just plain boring!

Use horizontally sliced bread loaves. Your sandwich yield will increase, and there will be less waste. Don't try to do this yourself. Your local bakery will be happy to slice your bread loaf to order.

Other Bites

For a lighter, less sweet version, especially during summer months when fruit is plentiful, substitute fresh peaches (peeled), figs, blueberries, or cherries for the dried fruit.

Cucumber and Shrimp Triangles

When you think of an elegant sandwich, the classic cucumber sandwich probably comes to mind. This version takes that elegance one step further by including a crowd pleaser: shrimp. Refreshing and easy to prepare, these sandwiches are for any party, large or small.

Yield: 16 sandwiches

⅓ cup shredded cucumber, well drained

1 cup shrimp, cooked and chopped

2 teaspoons green onion, minced

1½ teaspoons lemon juice

⅛ teaspoon dill

¼ cup plain yogurt

Salt and black pepper to taste

8 slices firm white bread

4 tablespoons butter, softened

Extra plain yogurt, for garnish

¾ cup parsley, finely minced, as garnish

Spread bread slices thinly with butter and thoroughly mix all other ingredients. Spread filling equally on 4 slices. Top with remaining slices. Cut off crusts, then cut each sandwich into triangles.

Using a small metal spatula, spread a thin layer of yogurt on the edges of each sandwich and press the edges into the chopped parsley leaves.

Little Bits

Chop the garnish finely when preparing for a decorative edge. The smaller the pieces, the more likely the garnish will adhere.

Other Bites

Substitute chunk tuna or chopped chicken for an easy variation.

Curry Cashew Bites

Make a culinary statement. Using the primary ingredients of each sandwich to garnish the edges is an attractive way to let your guests know what is inside before they take a bite.

Yield: 24 sandwiches

8 ounces cream cheese, softened

3 tablespoons milk

3 teaspoons curry powder (or less if desired)

¾ cup finely chopped cashews

16 slices firm whole wheat bread

1 ounce cream cheese

2 tablespoons milk

1 cup cashews, finely chopped, as garnish

Using a wooden spoon, cream 8 ounces cream cheese and 3 tablespoons milk in a small bowl. Stir in the curry and cashews until combined.

In a separate small bowl, mix the extra cream cheese and milk together. Reserve for garnishing.

Spread the cashew filling equally on 8 slices of bread. Top with remaining bread slices, then cut the crusts off with a sharp knife. Cut each sandwich into thirds (3 equal rectangles).

Using a small spatula or knife, coat one end of each sandwich and about a quarter of the edge along the length of it with the milk and cream cheese; press the coated sandwich tip into the extra cashews so each sandwich has one end covered with cashews.

Little Bits

Cutting the crusts off after the filling has been spread ensures clean, straight edges. A sharp, medium-weight or serrated knife works best.

Other Bites

While this curry flavor is very mild, think about other nut or spice combinations you might like to substitute: cayenne pepper for the curry, almonds for the cashews, or rosemary and walnuts.

Caper and Green Tea Squares

When you need an easy snack food, instead of chicken fingers, offer bite-size sandwiches. Your guests will gobble these up like popcorn!

Yield: 64 bite-size sandwiches

8 ounces (1 cup) whipped cream cheese

4 teaspoons green tea leaves

4 teaspoons small capers, drained and rinsed

1 tablespoon hot water (or more, if needed)

4 tablespoons minced shallots

8 slices firm bread, 4 white and 4 whole wheat

Combine the cream cheese, tea, capers, and hot water in a food processor and pulse until smooth, adding just enough water to smooth out the mixture. Scrape into a small bowl and stir in the shallots. Cover and chill until needed.

Spread the caper filling evenly over 4 slices of white bread, then top with remaining bread slices. Cut off all crusts, then cut each sandwich into sixteen ½ to ¾-inch sandwich bites.

Little Bits

Toasting the bread first adds texture. Save time by filling a baking sheet with bread slices and baking in the oven at 375°F.

Other Bites

Capers have a wonderful bite, but if you want a milder flavor, substitute chopped parsley or finely chopped, seeded tomato for the capers.

Center: Tarragon Egg Boxes, page 60; middle: English Style Potted Ham Shapes, page 44; front: Smoked Salmon Hearts, page 26; Jamaican Beef Turnovers, page 70.

Cutter-Shaped Sandwiches

Put your Christmas cookie cutters to use all year-round with these distinctive sandwich shapes and inlay ideas. They take only a few seconds more!

- Cucumber Apricot Flowers
- Smoked Salmon Hearts
- Fiesta Chicken Squares
- Confetti Spread Butterflies
- Bacon Chutney Tulips
- Tea-Smoked Egg Diamonds

Cucumber Apricot Flowers

Fresh apricots are bold in color yet delicate in flavor. When paired with these ingredients, however, they make these unassuming sandwiches really stand out.

Yield: 24 sandwiches

8 ounces farmers or marscapone cheese, softened

¼ cup fresh basil, finely snipped

¼ teaspoon salt

24 slices firm white bread

3 slices firm whole wheat bread

1 cup arugula

4 large apricots, pitted and thinly sliced

2 large cucumbers, peeled and thinly sliced

Flower-shaped cutter measuring about 2½ inches

Small round cutter measuring about ¾ inch

In a small bowl, combine cheese, basil, and salt.

Cut out 2 flowers from each white bread slice, for a total of 48 pieces. Using the small circle cutter, cut out the center of half of the flower-shaped slices and set the centers aside. Then, using the same cutter, cut out 24 circles from the 3 whole wheat slices. Insert these circles into the white bread holes to create a brown center for half the flowers. You will now have 24 whole white flower slices and 24 with brown centers.

To assemble the sandwiches, spread about 1 tablespoon of the herbed cheese on one side of all 24 flowers. Then, using each solid white slice for the base, place a leaf or two of arugula on top of the filling, top with apricot and cucumber slices, and place the two-toned bread flower on top.

----------- ⟲ -----------

Little Bits

Cucumbers are 96% water. To ensure that your sandwiches don't get soggy, spread the cucumber slices on a paper towel to drain for a few minutes. Then pat the tops dry before assembling the sandwiches. Use English cucumbers if you can find them; they have fewer seeds.

Other Bites

For an exotic flavor, use finely sliced water chestnuts (patted dry with a paper towel) in place of cucumbers. A thin slice of jicama can also add a nice crunch.

Smoked Salmon Hearts

An easy and contemporary take on bagels and lox!

Yield: 16 sandwiches

8 tablespoons butter, softened

1 small shallot, finely chopped

4 tablespoons chopped fresh tarragon or dill

8 slices firm white bread

10 ounces smoked salmon

6 ounces cream cheese, softened

1 teaspoon fresh lemon juice

Fresh-ground black pepper

16 slices firm white bread

Heart-shaped cutter measuring about 2 inches

Heart-shaped aspic cutter measuring about ¾ inch

In a small bowl, combine butter with shallots and herbs. Mix well. Cut 2 heart shapes out of each bread slice to make thirty-two 2-inch hearts. Spread 16 with herb butter. Carefully cut out a small heart shape in the center of these hearts using the aspic cutter. Spread cream cheese on the other 16 hearts.

Lay slices of smoked salmon on top of the cream cheese. Sprinkle the salmon with lemon juice and ground pepper. Press the herb-coated bread slices on top to form 16 sandwiches.

———————— ⟲ ————————

Little Bits

Feel free to experiment with breads dyed various colors. By working closely with your local bakery, you can make sure you get just the color you want, not some unexpected neon surprise!

Other Bites

Layer slices of pimento on top of a thin layer of cream cheese mixed with chopped sage as another option.

Fiesta Chicken Squares

For this fun recipe, pretend you are putting together a puzzle.
The texture of the bread will hold the shapes together.

Yield: 24 small sandwiches

4 skinless, boneless chicken breasts, cooked and finely chopped (about 3 cups)

1 medium shallot, peeled and minced

½ green pepper, finely chopped

½ yellow or orange pepper, finely chopped

1 large tomato, skin removed, seeded and finely chopped
(drained, canned tomatoes are acceptable)

3 tablespoons mayonnaise

⅛ teaspoon cumin

½ teaspoon oregano

½ teaspoon salt

20 slices firm white bread (avoid thinly-sliced bread for this recipe)

8 slices firm whole wheat bread (avoid thinly-sliced bread for this recipe)

1 teaspoon minced jalapeño pepper, seeds removed

4 tablespoons butter, softened

1 square cutter measuring 2¼ inches

1 square cutter measuring 1¼ inches

1 square cutter measuring ¾ inch

Mix the chicken, shallot, pepper, tomato, mayonnaise, and spices in a medium-sized bowl. Refrigerate until ready to use.

Take 9 slices of the white bread and, with the 2¼-inch cutter, cut 4 squares out of each slice to yield a total of 36 squares. Take the 4 whole wheat slices and, with the 1¼-inch cutter, cut 3 squares from each slice to yield 12 squares total.

Take 12 of the white bread squares and the 12 whole wheat squares and, with the 1¼-inch cutter, cut a square out of each to yield twenty-four 2¼-inch "frames" with 1⅜-inch "windows." Finally, take the twenty-four 1¼-inch squares you just made and, using the smallest cutter, cut a square center out of each.

You should now have 24 solid 2¼-inch squares, twenty-four 2¼-inch frames, twenty-four 1¼-inch frames, and 24 small square centers: enough shapes to create concentrically inlayed sandwiches

Assemble the pieces by laying alternatively colored breads inside each other. This should yield 12 white bread frames with a smaller whole wheat frame inside and a white center, and 12 bread frames with the reverse: a whole wheat outer frame, a smaller white bread inside, and a whole wheat center.

You should now have 24 sandwich tops that look like square dart boards. Spread a very thin layer of butter on each solid slice and top with the fiesta chicken mix. Top each sandwich with the geometric layer to make 24 sandwiches.

Little Bits

Use similarly-weighted breads to ensure uniformly-shaped sandwiches.

If you are having difficulty cutting the chicken into small pieces, pulse all filling ingredients briefly in a food processor until somewhat smooth but still chunky.

Other Bites

For a quicker filling alternative, use pre-cooked chicken slices with a layer of good salsa.

Confetti Spread Butterflies

Flecked with minced vegetables, this spread contrasts well with the dark bread, making it as pretty as it is tasty. The whimsical butterfly motif makes this the perfect bridal shower sandwich or afternoon tea accompaniment.

Yield: 24 sandwiches

8 ounces farmers cheese, softened (cream cheese is a good substitute)

½ cup each zucchini, orange pepper, and yellow pepper, finely diced

½ cup tomato, seeded and finely diced

Milk

Salt and fresh black pepper

18 slices dense dark bread

Caviar, as garnish

Bean sprouts, as garnish

Pastry bag fitted with a ½-inch round tip

Round cutter measuring 1½ inches

Mix the vegetables and the farmers cheese until smooth. A drop of milk may be needed to create a spreadable texture. Salt and pepper to taste.

Cut 3 rounds from each slice of bread for a total of 36 rounds, then use a sharp knife to cut 12 of the rounds into quarters. Set these aside.

Thinly spread the sandwich mixture onto the remaining 24 uncut rounds. Fill the pastry bag with the remaining filling. For each sandwich, pipe the filling into a cigar shape for the butterfly body; then press 2 cut bread triangles into the body on an angle to create the wings. With the tip of a knife or spoon, add some caviar to one end of the body to form a head. Press 2 bean sprouts into the end to serve as antennae. Serve immediately.

If you want to make these in advance, assemble the sandwiches but don't add the caviar until the last minute, as it will bleed into your filling.

———————— 6 ————————

Little Bits

Get fancy. Using small aspic cutters, cut designs into the wings to create a lace effect.

Other Bites

A good tuna fish filling can be used for the butterfly body, and capers can be used in place of the caviar for the butterfly head.

Bacon Chutney Tulips

A classic English savory, Devils on Horseback, inspired this sandwich. The harmony of ingredients creates a completely new flavor that defies description and is entirely different from the individual ingredient flavors.

Yield: 24 sandwiches

1 cup pitted prunes, cut into small pieces

½ cup fruit chutney, finely chopped

1½ cups grated sharp cheddar cheese

10 strips bacon, cooked crisp and crumbled

12 slices firm egg bread, toasted (challah works well)

Tulip-shaped cutter measuring about 1½ x 2½ inches

Combine prunes, chutney, cheese, and bacon in a small bowl.

Spread filling on 6 slices of bread, place the remaining bread on top, and cut 2 shapes out of each sandwich. Reserve the remaining bread pieces for future use.

Little Bits

When choosing cutter shapes for sandwiches, keep the design simple. Bread edges will look ragged if your cutters have a fluted edge, so choose straight-sided cutters when available.

Other Bites

Mix any chutney with cream cheese and omit the prunes and bacon to create a smooth spread.

Tea-Smoked Egg Diamonds

After eating at Silver Tips Tea Room in Tarrytown, N.Y., I fell in love with their smoky-flavored egg salad. By the following summer, I had figured out a close reproduction, using Lapsong Souchong tea and star anise.

Yield: 16 sandwiches

8 large eggs

2 tablespoons kosher salt

4 tablespoons dark soy sauce

4 whole star anise pods

3 tablespoons Lapsong Souchong tea (available in any grocery store)

2 tablespoons mayonnaise (optional)

2 tablespoons minced fresh parsley

1 teaspoon dijon mustard

1 teaspoon fresh lemon juice

⅛ teaspoon salt

Fresh-ground black pepper to taste

8 to 12 slices pumpernickel bread

Diamond-shaped cutter measuring 1 to 1½ inches

To make the eggs, boil in a medium saucepan for 12 minutes. Drain and let cool another 15 minutes. Using a wooden spoon or by gently rapping them on a countertop, tap the egg shells until they are cracked all over.

In a medium saucepan, combine the salt, soy sauce, star anise, and tea. Add the eggs and enough water to cover the eggs by 1 inch of water. Bring to a boil and simmer gently for 2 hours, adding more water if needed. Remove from heat and let the eggs stand, still immersed, for another hour. Drain and let eggs cool completely before peeling and dicing them finely.

For the filling, mix eggs, mayonnaise, parsley, mustard, lemon juice, salt, and pepper together in a medium-sized bowl.

Depending on the size of the bread slices, you should be able to cut at least 3 diamond shapes out of each slice. Cut 32 diamond shapes, then use a spatula to carefully spread the egg salad on 16 of them. Top with the remaining diamonds.

Little Bits

Avoid using a typical cookie cutter: most are too shallow. Professional cutter sets will cut cleanly through two layers of bread with filling.

Other Bites

Regular hard-boiled eggs and finely minced chives make a tasty alternative.

From left: Stilton Pear Bites, page 46; Caviar-Tipped Rolls, page 64; Beef, Apple, and Watercress Spirals, page 38; Fiesta Chicken Squares, page 28; Mock Crab Flowers, page 42.

Open-Faced Sandwiches

The challenge of open-faced sandwiches is to make them look appetizing and attractive. You don't want a "glob" of filling dropped onto a slice of bread. These small, open-faced sandwiches each have their own distinct style, flavor, and garnish.

- Beef, Apple, and Watercress Spirals
- Austrian Cheese Triangles
- Mock Crab Flowers
- English Style Potted Ham Shapes
- Stilton Pear Bites

Beef, Apple, & Watercress Spirals

When my niece was just a little girl, my sister helped her celebrate New Year's by making simple hors d'oeuvres of rolled ham and cheese spirals, pierced with a fancy toothpick and served at midnight. I never forgot my niece's excitement over her New Year's Eve party. Little did she know they had turned the clocks forward so that "midnight" came at 8 p.m.! I have used the rolled meat idea for this open sandwich.

Yield: 30 sandwiches

½ cup plain low-fat yogurt

2 tablespoons creamy horseradish sauce

1½ teaspoons lime juice

½ teaspoon fresh-ground black pepper

1 apple, cored and sliced into small, matchstick-size pieces

1 tablespoon lemon juice

1 bunch watercress, thick stalks removed, chopped

6 slices roast beef, sliced medium thickness

15 slices firm whole grain bread

Round cutter measuring 1½ inches

In a small bowl, toss the apple pieces with lemon juice. Set aside. Combine the yogurt, horseradish sauce, lime juice, and pepper in a small bowl.

Cut 2 rounds from each slice of bread for a total of 30 rounds. Wrap in plastic to keep from drying out, and set aside.

Spread a thin layer of the yogurt-horseradish on a slice of roast beef. Sprinkle the surface with the chopped watercress, then carefully place the apple sticks in a line across the narrow bottom edge of the roast beef slice. As you would a jelly roll, roll the meat over the apple and continue to the opposite edge to create a beef roll. Using a sharp knife, cut the roll into 5 equal slices.

Place 1 slice of beef roll on top of each bread circle (you may need to anchor it with a dab of the yogurt spread). Top the slice with a few watercress leaves and serve.

Little Bits

The beef slices must be at least ⅛-inch thick or your roll will not hold together and your spiral will look flimsy when sliced. Ask your local deli to slice the roast beef thick enough roll easily.

Other Bites

Create the elegant rolled sandwich pictured on page 62. Take one slice of marbled bread and cut into a 3-inch square. Press the bread flat with a rolling pin. Lay a slice of roast beef on top, along with a thin layer of yogurt spread. Arrange 1 tablespoon of apple pieces and 3 sprigs of watercress along one edge of the bread. Make sure the leafy portion of the watercress is protruding from one end. Dampen the opposite end of the bread. Starting on the apple-watercress end, roll the bread up like a jelly roll. Press the bread seam together gently. Stand upright on a small plate and serve.

For a more sophisticated flavor combination, use an herbed cheese spread and replace apple with crispy onion rings and the watercress with arugula.

Austrian Cheese Triangles

One year I helped cater a holiday party for the Lincoln Center Library in New York. The good news is I discovered this fantastic spread. The bad news is that I ate nearly half of the bowl before the guests arrived. The caraway gives this spread its unique flavor, made especially delicious with dark bread.

Yield: 32 sandwiches

4 ounces softened butter

8 ounces quark (also known as curd cheese) or softened cream cheese

2 teaspoons grated onion

1 teaspoon Dijon mustard

1 tablespoon ground caraway seeds

1 tablespoon chopped parsley

1 teaspoon chopped chives

1 tablespoon sweet paprika

¼ teaspoon salt

Ground black pepper to taste

8 slices dark bread

Chopped chives or caraway seeds, as garnish

Pastry bag fitted with a ½-inch star tip

Combine all ingredients until smooth, except the bread and extra chives. Using a serrated knife, cut the crusts off the bread slices making sure each slice is a perfect square. Spread a thin coating of filling on each slice, cut into equal size triangles for a total of 32 open-faced sandwiches.

Fill the pastry bag and decoratively pipe small even stars of filling over each triangle surface. Depending on your taste, sprinkle a few caraway seeds or chives on top.

Little Bits

Don't have a pastry bag? Fill a plastic bag with filling. Securely close the bag and cut a small tip from one corner. Squeeze random squiggles of filling over the surface.

Other Bites

Use flexible butter molds to mold the cheese spread into shapes. Freeze the filled molds for easy removal. Place the sculpted cheese shape on top of a bread shape and garnish with a few chive stalks and a sprinkle of caraway seeds.

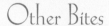

Mock Crab Flowers

I found this 1940's sandwich in my grandmother's recipe collection. While the spread is pink like crab, it actually tastes nothing like seafood. This retro recipe is a tasty and colorful choice to add to any sandwich assortment.

Yield: 24 sandwiches

⅔ cup grated cheddar cheese

⅔ cup finely chopped hard boiled eggs (3 to 4 eggs)

⅔ cup finely diced, seeded tomato

1 teaspoon vegetable oil

Lemon juice

Salt and black pepper

Tabasco sauce

Unsalted butter, softened

12 slices firm white bread

1 medium ripe tomato, as garnish

Dill sprigs, as garnish

Flower-shaped cutter measuring 2 to 2½ inches

Round aspic cutter measuring about ¾ inches

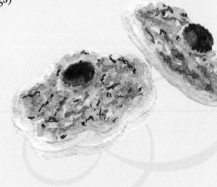

In a small bowl mix the cheese, egg, and tomato. Moisten with vegetable oil and a drop or two of lemon juice. Season with salt, black pepper, and Tabasco sauce to taste.

Spread a thin coating of butter over all of the bread slices. Keeping in mind that most standard-size bread slices will only yield 2 flower shapes, spread the mock crab filling over the 12 slices, focusing on the areas where the cutter will cut out the flower image; there is less waste that way. Using the flower cutter, cut 2 sandwiches out of each slice topped with filling. You may need to rinse off the cutter from time to time to ensure clean cuts.

To prepare the garnish (flower centers), use a sharp paring knife to carefully cut the tomato in half vertically and scrape away the tomato interior, leaving 2 hollow tomato halves. Cutting a few slits in the edges, flatten the curved tomato skins. Press the round aspic cutter into the skin and cut out 24 tomato circles. Place the flower centers skin side up in the center of each crab flower sandwich. Add a sprig of dill on the side of each flower to represent a leaf.

Little Bits

Use thinly sliced, firm bread. The ratio of filling to bread is the key to a great tasting sandwich.

Other Bites

Use a wide-tipped pastry bag to pipe the filling onto each sandwich. Just remember that if your filling is chunky it may get stuck if your tip isn't wide enough.

English Style Potted Ham Shapes

ATTENTION: Potted ham is not SPAM! Before refrigeration existed, it was traditional to seal a crock or bowl of spiced meat with melted butter, hence the name "potted." And in fact, this easy spread tastes better made a few days in advance. The fact that there's a bit of sherry included only adds to the punning fun!

Yield: 24 sandwiches

½ pound ham, cut into chunks

2 tablespoons mayonnaise

1 tablespoon Dijon mustard

2 teaspoons horseradish

Salt and fresh-ground black pepper

½ cup (1 stick) unsalted butter

3 tablespoons minced gherkins (cornichons)

2 tablespoons sherry

12 slices rye bread

Small gherkins, sliced, as garnish

Place the ham, mayonnaise, mustard, and horseradish in a food processor and pulse until smooth. Add the butter and process until combined. Season with salt and black pepper.

Scrape the mixture into a medium-sized bowl. Fold the minced gherkins into the filling. Cover the bowl and refrigerate for at least 24 hours.

Toast the bread. Cut 2 shapes out of each slice, for a total of 24 hexagons. Spread the filling over the surface and top with a small gherkin as a garnish.

Little Bits

Bread shapes can always be cut in advance. Kept in airtight containers; they will keep refrigerated for a week or frozen for one month.

Other Bites

Give your filling a kick in the pickles! Replace the gherkins with a tablespoon of minced, seeded jalapeños, omit the sherry, and replace the ground black pepper with ⅛ teaspoon of cloves. Garnish with other small tasty tidbits: capers, finely chopped bits of colored pepper, pimento cut into shapes, chopped celery leaves, or sprigs of thyme.

Stilton Pear Bites

I'm a firm believer that Americans do not eat enough pears. We seem to favor the apple in both sweet and savory dishes. This sandwich is a perfect example of how pears, cheese, and black pepper merge to create the perfect savory bite.

Yield: 16 sandwiches

4 slices pumpernickel bread, toasted

1 cup small watercress sprigs, thick stems removed

1 ripe pear, cored and sliced thinly

4 ounces Stilton cheese

Juice of half a lemon

Fresh-ground black pepper

Preheat oven to 400°F. Cut off bread crusts and cut each slice into 4 squares. Arrange the 16 squares in a single layer in a heatproof dish or shallow baking pan. Layer the watercress sprigs and half of the pear slices over each toasted square. Crumble the Stilton over the pears.

In a small bowl, toss the remaining slices of pear with the lemon juice to prevent them from discoloring and set aside.

Bake the toast slices for 10 minutes or until the cheese is melted and bubbling. Garnish with remaining pear slices. Grind a little black pepper over each and serve warm.

Little Bits

When mounding the filling onto a precut bread shape, leave a little room around the edges to "frame" your filling with the exposed bread edge.

Other Bites

For an easy and elegant presentation, use a few perfect pears of different kinds, colors, and shapes to create a small still life of pears and thyme sprigs in the center of your platter, arranging your sandwiches around the perimeter.

From left: Olive Spread Pinwheels, page 52; Austrian Cheese Triangles, page 40; Cucumber Apricot Sandwiches (hexagon/heart variation), page 24.

Rolled, Stacked, and Carved Sandwiches

Creative sandwich shapes give tasty fillings exponential appeal. A platter featuring an assortment of pinwheels, multi-layered sandwiches, and other unusual shapes is simply irresistible.

- Avocado Pine Nut Layers
- Olive Spread Pinwheels
- Hummus Stacks
- Herbed Cheese Gift Boxes
- Tomato-Eyed Pyramids
- Tarragon Egg Boxes

Avocado Pine Nut Layers

The filling in this recipe is based on an old Pueblo recipe. This Native American version of guacamole is a delight, even for those who don't like avocados!

Yield: 24 sandwiches

2 ripe avocados

Juice of 1 lemon

Juice of 1 lime

1 cup chopped pine nuts (walnuts or cashews can be substituted)

1 firm tomato, cored, seeded, and finely chopped

3 scallions, sliced thin and minced

½ clove garlic, peeled and finely minced

¼ teaspoon crushed coriander seed

¼ teaspoon fresh-ground black pepper

1 teaspoon Worcestershire sauce

¼ teaspoon Tabasco sauce

¼ teaspoon salt

10 slices firm white bread

4 slices pumpernickel or firm dark bread

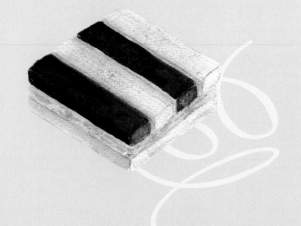

Halve the avocados, remove the pit, and scoop the flesh into a medium-sized bowl. Toss the avocado with the lemon and lime juice to prevent browning, then pulse the avocado in a food processor once or twice to chop the avocado. Scrape the chopped avocado back into the bowl and add the remaining ingredients. Stir to combine.

Stack the bread slices, 3 to 4 at a time, to cut off the crusts and to ensure all the bread is of equal size, about 3½-inches square. Cut 6 white slices into quarters, creating 24 squares, and set aside. Layer the remaining slices of bread into 2 stacks of 4 slices, alternating the breads.

Spread just enough of the avocado filling between the layers of the mixed bread stacks so the 4 layers stick together. Use a serrated knife to cut each rectangle into 6 striped slices. Cut each slice in half to create 12 striped sandwich tops.

Spread the remaining filling equally on each sandwich bottom. Top with striped slices to create 24 sandwiches.

Little Bits

If you choose to experiment, don't confuse flavors in your sandwich. Use the same filling or flavor for your sandwich mortar as you do for the filling.

Other Bites

Fill your sandwich with a nut spread like Nutella and glue your top layer together with a good jam. Result: an adult nut butter & jelly sandwich!

Olive Spread Pinwheels

In the 1950s, this style of sandwich was very popular. They look great, are very easy to prepare, and yield a lot with little effort. Great for a small tea or a large crowd!

Yield: 24 sandwiches

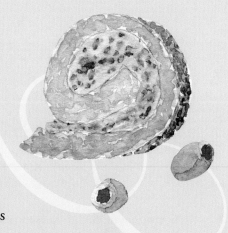

4 tablespoons unsalted butter, softened

1 small shallot, finely chopped

1 teaspoon chopped fresh rosemary or thyme

1 cup pimento-stuffed green olives, finely chopped

1 teaspoon fresh lemon juice

4 ounces cream cheese, softened

4 slices whole wheat bread, sliced to measure 6 x 4 inches

Sprigs of watercress, as garnish

In a small bowl, combine the butter, shallots, and herb. Mix well. Add the chopped olives and lemon juice; combine. Using rolling pin, lightly flatten bread slices. Spread a thin layer of cream cheese over each slice, then spread ¼ of the olive filling onto each slice, leaving a ½-inch space at the edge.

Place each bread slice on top of a piece of plastic wrap. Using the edge of the plastic wrap to help you, start at one short side and tightly roll the slice up, pressing firmly, until you reach the other end. Repeat until all bread slices are rolled. Wrap in plastic wrap and chill.

When ready to serve, unwrap and slice each roll into 5 slices. Garnish with watercress sprigs.

Little Bits

The sandwiches in this chapter can be made up to 12 hours in advance, placed on a tray, and covered with a damp kitchen towel. Keep refrigerated until ready to serve.

Other Bites

In a rush? Just use any good jar of bruschetta topping. But do spread a layer of butter or cream cheese on the bread surface before you roll it up. The butter will give the filling "something sticky" to hang onto.

Hummus Stacks

I don't know why, but I love chickpeas. For once I crave a healthy food! This is a firmer spread than traditional hummus and great for those vegetarians in your crowd.

Yield: 48 sandwiches

1 large clove garlic, finely chopped (about 1 tablespoon)

15 ounces cooked chickpeas (garbanzo beans), drained

¼ cup natural, smooth peanut butter

¼ cup fresh lemon juice

Salt and black pepper

6 slices bread, 4 dark multigrain and 2 firm white

Using a food processor, mix the garlic, chickpeas, peanut butter, and lemon juice until smooth and spreadable. Season with salt and pepper.

Make 2 stacks of bread, each with a white slice in the center. Cut the crusts off to make the slices uniformly square. Take 1 whole grain and 1 white slice from each stack and spread ¼ of the hummus mixture on each. Press the remaining whole wheat slice on top of each stack to create 2 double-decker sandwiches. Wrap the stacks in plastic wrap and chill until firm.

Using a sharp serrated knife, carefully cut each sandwich stack into 6 even slices, then cut those slices in half, creating 24 small striped sandwiches. Serve on their side with the layered bread and hummus exposed.

Hummus holds up well refrigerated for 4 to 5 days and can be frozen in an airtight container, so feel free to make extra.

Little Bits

Chilling any stacked or pinwheel sandwiches in the refrigerator or briefly in the freezer prior to slicing will give you a cleaner, neater slice.

Other Bites

Add ½ cup drained roasted red peppers, finely chopped sun-dried tomatoes, or ½ cup chopped parsley to change the color and add another dimension of flavor. For those who must have meat in their dishes, add pieces of chopped chicken or turkey.

Herbed Cheese Gift Boxes

I have always loved those soft, creamy (and expensive) herb cheeses one finds in the specialty cheese section of the grocery store, and I could easily devour a whole little tub with just a bunch of carrot sticks. I had to find a cheaper and simpler version to satisfy my cravings. This recipe is the result.

Yield: 32 sandwiches

8 ounces whipped cream cheese

4 to 6 tablespoons crème fraîche (yogurt or milk can be substituted)

1 small clove garlic, finely chopped

4 to 6 tablespoons herbs, finely chopped: parsley, chives, marjoram, tarragon, and/or basil

Salt and black pepper to taste

10 slices firm whole wheat or dark bread (not white)

Curly parsley, as garnish

In a small bowl, combine all the ingredients with a spatula. Add salt and pepper to taste. Let this mixture rest for a few hours at room temperature to enhance the flavor.

Spread the filling evenly over 8 slices of bread. Remove the crusts and cut each slice into 4 squares for a total of 32 squares. Cut the remaining 2 slices into squares as well, then cut each of these squares into three ¼-inch x 1-inch strips. These will form the "ribbon."

Place one strip across another in an "X" and press in the center so they stick together. Place this cross on top of the filling and add a parsley leaf at the center for a "bow." Repeat for each sandwich.

Little Bits

If the bread you are using is too thick or firm, pressing the "X" together may not work. You can still create the cross by cutting one of the strips in half and laying each half on opposite sides of the other strip.

Other Bites

Use thin slices of carrot, pepper, or chive to create a pattern on top of each square to serve as the "bow."

Tomato-Eyed Pyramids

I have used this filling for bruschetta and as an hors d'oeuvre topping, but the olive bread framing this sandwich makes it an original: a sophisticated flavor combination in a unique sandwich presentation.

Yield: 32 sandwiches

1 cup oil-packed sun dried tomatoes, drained

12 ounces roasted sweet red peppers, drained

1 packed cup fresh basil leaves

½ cup walnuts, toasted

1 tablespoon balsamic vinegar

2 large garlic cloves

1½ teaspoons grated lemon peel

1 loaf olive bread, unsliced

Salt and black pepper

Round cutter measuring ¾ inch

Pastry bag fitted with a plain tip about ¾-inch wide

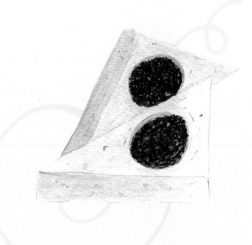

Chop all ingredients (except for the bread) in a food processor to make a coarse paste. Season with salt and pepper to taste and set the mixture aside.

Cut the loaf into a crustless rectangle measuring 3½ x 3½ x 11 inches. Freeze the loaf to make slicing easier.

Standing the loaf on the square end, cut the loaf in an "X" pattern into 4 triangular loaves. Cut each loaf into 12 triangles, each ¾-inch thick. Cut a circle out of the center of each triangle using the round cutter.

Fill a pastry bag, fitted with the ¾-inch round tip, with the tomato mixture. Lay the bread triangles on a baking sheet lined with plastic wrap and pipe the filling into the holes you have just created. The filling will cover any ragged edges, making a round red center. Once filled, these sandwiches can be frozen in an airtight container for up to two weeks. Bring to room temperature before serving.

Little Bits

Choose a uniformly-textured bread for this sculpted sandwich. Breads with lots of large holes will look too ragged when cut.

Other Bites

Almost any filling, chunky or smooth, will work in this sandwich.

Tarragon Egg Boxes

Tarragon is the key to this recipe. It is an herb the French use frequently, but the American palate is not as accustomed to its delicate, faintly licorice flavor. Tarragon transforms everyday eggs into a palate-pleasing delight, and the toast box containers make for perfect brunch or party fare.

Yield: 32 boxes

1 loaf white bread, unsliced, with crusts removed

Vegetable oil for brushing

8 large eggs

¼ cup minced fresh tarragon

½ cup minced scallion, including the light green part

¼ cup milk

Salt and black pepper to taste

3 tablespoons unsalted butter

Tarragon sprigs, as garnish

To make the bread cubes, cut the loaf into a rectangle measuring 3 x 3 x 12 inches. Cut the loaf lengthwise in half, and then cut each half in half so that you end up with 4 loaves, each measuring an 1½-inch square in cross section. Cut these loaves into 8 equal 1½-inch "slices," each forming a cube. Take a small paring knife and cut a well about halfway down into each cube and about ¾-inch across.

Using a small pastry brush, brush cube edges with oil and place cubes on an unlined baking sheet. Bake at 350°F for 10 minutes or until the bread is toasted. Remove from the oven to cool. These bread boxes can be prepared in advance and stored in an airtight container in a cool place for 3 to 4 days.

In a bowl, whisk together the eggs, minced tarragon, scallion, milk, salt, and pepper. In a heavy saucepan, melt the butter over moderate heat until it is foamy, add the egg mixture, and reduce the heat to low. Cook the egg, stirring occasionally with a whisk, for 3 to 5 minutes, or until just set. The scrambled eggs should have small curds and appear very creamy.

When ready to serve, fill the cavities of the bread cubes with the egg and garnish with tarragon sprigs. Serve warm.

Little Bits

Make friends with your local bakery so you can order, on short notice, loaves of uncut bread. Or you can order more in advance and freeze it; just remember to put wax paper or parchment paper between the slices before freezing so you can take what you need and not defrost an entire loaf if it is not needed.

Other Bites

These toasted bread cubes are very sturdy. Fill them with any leftovers, hot or cold; just be sure to chop any large pieces so the mixture fits easily into the well of the cube.

Beef, Apple, and Watercress Spirals, page 39.

Pressed & Shaped Sandwiches

Bread is a versatile, readily available staple that can be used in the most inventive and tasty ways. All that is needed is a little moisture by way of melted butter or oil to help create the shapes for these unconventional sandwiches, all inspired by bread-based desserts I learned to make at the French Culinary Institute.

- Caviar-Tipped Rolls
- Grape, Brie, and Walnut Cups
- Peach Scallop and Ceviche Tulips
- Jamaican Beef Turnovers

Caviar-Tipped Rolls

These delicate cigarette-shaped sandwiches are an easy accompaniment to wine with friends, yet sophisticated enough for the most elaborate affair.

Yield: 16 rolls

8 eggs, hard boiled and cooled

1½ tablespoons sour cream

1½ tablespoons mayonnaise

¼ teaspoon salt

¼ teaspoon white pepper

8 slices firm white bread, crusts removed

4 ounces black lumpfish caviar, as garnish

Extra sour cream or mayonnaise, as garnish

Blend the cooked eggs, sour cream, mayonnaise, salt, and pepper in a food processor until smooth and creamy. Scoop the mixture into a medium-sized bowl and fold 1 tablespoon of caviar into the egg mixture.

Using a rolling pin, flatten the bread slices. Spread equal amounts of the egg filling over the surface of each bread slice, leaving 1½-inch strip of edge uncovered.

Roll each slice, in jelly roll fashion, creating 8 rolls. Cut each in half. Spread a little bit of sour cream or mayonnaise on the tip and ½ inch down the sides. Press and roll the creamed end into the caviar to cover. Serve immediately.

The rolled sandwiches can be prepared in advance and kept in an airtight container, but save garnishing the edges until just before they are served to prevent the caviar from bleeding.

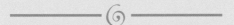

Little Bits

When making rolled sandwiches (logs), be sure to roll the bread very flat first, otherwise the sandwiches will be too chunky and difficult to roll. And be careful not to overfill; rolling logs or pinwheels naturally forces some of the filling out.

Other Bites

If caviar is too fancy or salty for your taste, tie a long chive into a bow around the middle, or cover the ends with finely chopped parsley or poppy seeds.

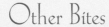

Grape, Brie, and Walnut Cups

I don't know when this filling has ever not been a sure-fire hit. The flavors meld to produce a delicious and distinctive savory.

Yield: 48 cups

24 slices bread or enough for 48 bread rounds

1 stick unsalted butter (4 ounces), melted

1 cup seedless grapes

2 tablespoons kosher salt

1 tablespoon finely chopped chives or scallions

1 tablespoon balsamic vinegar

2 teaspoons olive oil

¼ teaspoon fresh rosemary, chopped

¼ teaspoon minced garlic

¼ teaspoon fresh-ground black pepper

½ cup pecans, toasted and chopped

8 ounces Brie, rind removed, cut into small pieces

Miniature muffin pans

Round cutter measuring 1½ inches

Preheat the oven to 350°F. Using cutter, cut out 2 bread rounds from each slice of bread. Brush rounds with melted butter and carefully press into muffin pan cups. Bake for 12 minutes or until bread cups are toasted.

Pulse the grapes and the kosher salt in a food processor until the grapes are coarsely chopped. Transfer the mixture to a strainer placed over a bowl and let the mixture rest for about 15 minutes. Discard the drained liquid. In a small bowl, add the green onions, vinegar, oil, rosemary, garlic, and pepper to the grape mixture and mix well.

Sprinkle ½ teaspoon of nuts into each toasted bread cup; distribute the Brie equally between the 48 cups. Using a fork and making sure not to pick up too much liquid, fill each cup with the grape mixture. Bake the cups for 5 minutes or until the cheese mixture begins to melt. Serve immediately or at room temperature.

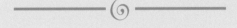

Little Bits

Bread cups can be made up to a week in advance, toasted, and stored in an airtight container. Fill just before serving.

Other Bites

Create a savory fruit salad to serve in these cups. Combine grapes, chopped strawberries and/or berries with balsamic vinegar sweetened with a little honey. The stickiness of the honey will help the fruit hold together, while the combination of honey and vinegar will add a sweet and sour dimension to the berries.

Peach Scallop Ceviche Tulips

So beautiful (and low in calories), this open bread "tulip cup" will take your guests' breath away! Don't worry, the lime juice "cooks" the scallops.

Yield: 18 tulip cups

1 cup peaches, peeled, pitted, and diced (about ¾ pound)

1 cup diced jicama

1 cup diced unpeeled English cucumber

1 cup small bay scallops (about ½ pound)

½ cup diced red pepper

⅓ cup chopped fresh cilantro

4 tablespoons fresh lime juice

2 tablespoons apricot preserves, finely chopped

27 slices firm white or whole wheat bread

Vegetable oil

Extra cilantro leaves, as garnish

18 cucumber slices, as garnish

Round cutter measuring 2½ inches

Miniature muffin pans

In a medium-sized bowl, combine all the ingredients except for the bread and oil. Set aside. The citric acid in the lime juice "cooks" the scallops by the time you need to fill the bread tulips.

Cut 2 rounds out of each bread slice to create 54 bread rounds. Using a pastry brush, brush each slice with oil. Press 3 rounds into each muffin cup, overlapping the edges to cover the bottom and sides of the tin. The rounded edges of the bread will extend above the surface, creating a petal-like edge. Press the bread into the tin so it forms a complete cup (with no holes).

Bake at 350°F for 8 to 12 minutes or until the bread cups are toasted. Be careful not to let the cup edges burn. Cool.

When ready to serve, use a slotted spoon to scoop and fill the bread tulips with the ceviche. Garnish with some cilantro and a slice of cucumber. Serve immediately. If you wait too long, the dampness of the filling will weaken the bottom of the cups, so do not assemble until just before serving.

Little Bits

Remember that the higher the bread protrudes above the top of the pan, the greater the risk of overbrowning or burning.

Other Bites

These bread cups can hold almost anything, sweet or savory. Any scoopable dessert or leftovers will work.

Jamaican Beef Turnovers

A classic spiced beef dish found in most major cities is transformed into a delicate sandwich turnover.

Yield: 48 turnovers

½ onion, finely chopped

1 scallion, finely chopped, including the white and light green parts

1 teaspoon finely chopped garlic

1 jalapeño pepper, seeded and minced

1 tablespoon oil

½ pound ground beef

1 teaspoon fresh thyme

1 teaspoon curry powder

½ teaspoon salt

¼ teaspoon black pepper

¼ cup unseasoned bread crumbs

24 slices firm white bread, crust trimmed off

8 tablespoons melted butter

In a small frying pan, sauté the onion, scallion, garlic and jalapeño pepper in oil until they are soft, about 3 minutes. Add the chopped beef and cook, stirring until the meat is browned. Add the remaining spices and continue to cook for another minute. If the mixture is very loose (depending on how fatty your beef is), add the bread crumbs to the mixture. This step may not be necessary, but the mixture must be able to hold together.

Using a rolling pin, flatten the bread slices. Cut each slice on the diagonal to create 2 triangles, 48 in all. Place a tablespoon of filling on one end of each triangle. Using a small pastry brush, wet all around the edges of one half, then fold the bread in half, lining the edges up to create a smaller triangle. Press the edges together with the tines of a fork. Repeat for all 48 triangles.

Preheat the oven to 350°F. Place the sandwich triangles on a parchment-lined baking sheet. Brush each triangle with butter and bake until toasted, about 10 minutes. Serve warm.

Little Bits

Depending on the density of the bread, you may need to press the middle down to fold the pockets without breaking.

Other Bites

Almost any meat or non-meat filling such as leftover chicken or chili can be used in these triangles; just make sure the filling you want to substitute is chopped finely and not too moist.

For a "grilled cheese" version, use sharp cheddar for the filling, with bacon bits if desired. Either way, kids love 'em!

Jam 'n Sponge Crosses, page 74.

Sweet Sandwiches

Sweet sandwiches? Why not? After all, what's peanut butter and jelly? Dessert sandwiches are the perfect way to top off a savory sandwich assortment. Here are a few ideas.

- Lime Curd Boxes
- Jam 'n Sponge Crosses
- Asian Pear Harvest Sandwiches
- Banana Morsels

Lime Curd Boxes

Light, and sweet, this unusual presentation for chiffon cake really amps up the wow factor.

Yield: 16 boxes

1¼ cup sifted cake flour

¾ cup granulated sugar, divided

1½ teaspoons baking powder

¼ teaspoon salt

3 large eggs, separated, at room temperature

⅓ cup water

¼ cup vegetable oil

1 teaspoon vanilla extract

1 large egg white

¼ teaspoon cream of tartar

½ cup lime juice

2 tablespoons lime zest

3 eggs

1½ cups sugar

⅛ teaspoon salt

8 tablespoons (1 stick) unsalted butter, melted

Mint leaves, as garnish

Melon baller

To make the cake, preheat oven to 325°F. Grease a 6 x 9-inch loaf pan and line with parchment paper.

Sift flour, ½ cup of the sugar, baking powder, and salt in a medium-sized bowl. Whisk together until well blended and set aside.

In a large bowl, whisk egg yolks, water, oil, and vanilla. Add dry ingredients ⅓ at a time, mixing until blended.

Using an electric mixer, beat egg whites and cream of tartar at medium speed until soft peaks form. Gradually beat in remaining ¼ cup sugar, then beat on high until whites are stiff. Using a rubber spatula, fold egg whites into batter in 2 to 3 stages. Scrape batter into loaf pan and smooth the top.

Bake for 30 minutes or until a cake tester inserted comes out clean. Place pan on a wire rack and loosen the cake with a knife. Cool for 15 minutes, remove cake and peel off parchment, then cool completely. Cake can be stored in an airtight container for 4 days.

To make the lime curd, mix juice zest, eggs, sugar, and salt in a blender for a few seconds. Then, with blender on low, carefully add melted butter. Pour into heavy saucepan and cook over medium heat, stirring constantly, until thickened. You should have about 1½ cups. Cover with a plastic wrap on the surface to prevent a skin from forming and cool.

To make the boxes, cut cake into a rectangle measuring 4 x 8 x 4 inches. Using a ruler if necessary, cut block in half along each dimension and again across its length to yield 16 2-inch cubes, keeping the sides of each cube straight and even.

To assemble, with the melon baller, scoop a well out from the top of each cube, being careful not to cut a hole in the base. Fill with lime curd and garnish with a mint leaf.

Little Bits

Cut the cake cubes in advance and keep frozen until ready to use. They thaw in minutes.

Other Bites

Fill cubes with pudding or whipped cream; include chopped fruit and nuts or raisins for added flavor. Also, toasting gives each bite a crispy crunch. Bake cubes at 350°F for 5 to 8 minutes until the edges are light brown, then fill.

Jam 'n Sponge Crosses

*These sweet little sandwiches are a modern version of
the Victorian Sponge, a teatime classic.*

Yield: 40 squares

1 cup butter (2 sticks), softened

1 cup strawberry jam

1 chiffon cake loaf measuring 3½ x 6 x 9 inches
(recipe on page 74)

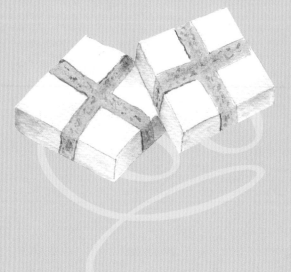

Using a hand mixer, cream the butter and strawberry jam in a small bowl until smooth. Set aside.

Trim cake loaf, removing all brown edges, so that it measures 3 x 4 x 8 inches. Cut in half horizontally, then cut those halves in half vertically along their length to create 4 mini loaves measuring 1½ x 2 x 8 inches each. Slice each loaf horizontally, once again to create a total of 8 pieces measuring ¾ x 2 x 8 inches.

Spread a thick (½-inch) layer of strawberry butter on 4 of the cake slices, then place the remaining slices on top to create 4 long sandwiches (measuring 1½ x 2 x 8 inches each). Cut each sandwich again vertically in half, lengthwise, through the filling. Spread another ½-inch layer of strawberry on each new cut piece. Press those pieces back together. You now have formed 4 "+" logs. Wrap each in plastic wrap and freeze. Slice each "+" log into 10 slices measuring ¾-inch thick, giving you a total of 40 sandwiches.

Little Bits

Too little filling will often cause sandwiches to fall apart, especially these. Be sure to have sufficient filling and to spread it evenly.

To ensure that your long pieces are cut evenly, use a serrated knife and place toothpicks as guides so your knife cuts will be consistent.

Other Bites

Butter can be flavored with almost any jam or crushed fresh fruit. For an even sweeter slice, a heavy butter cream frosting can be used as well.

Asian Pear Harvest Sandwiches

The richness of the brioche and the sweetened cheese makes these delightful as dessert or with a cup of tea.

Yield: 24 sandwiches

8 ounces cream cheese, softened

2 tablespoons brown sugar

½ teaspoon cinnamon

¼ teaspoon nutmeg

¼ teaspoon vanilla

2 Asian pears, cored, unpeeled

Lemon juice

1 loaf rich brioche, sliced to yield 12 slices, ½ to ¾-inch thick

4 ounces cream cheese

2 tablespoons milk

1 cup walnuts, chopped, toasted, as garnish

Combine 8 ounces cream cheese, brown sugar, cinnamon, nutmeg, and vanilla in a small bowl. Beat at medium speed with an electric mixer 1 minute or until smooth. Set aside.

Slice pears thinly and brush with lemon juice. Spread the cheese mixture evenly between the bread slices. Place pear slices on top of 6 of the slices and top with the remaining bread (cream cheese side down).

With a sharp knife, cut away the crust, then cut each sandwich diagonally twice to create 4 triangles.

In a separate small bowl, mix 4 ounces cream cheese with 2 tablespoons milk to create a thin paste. Lightly spread this on the sandwich edges and press edges into chopped nuts to create a decorative edge.

Little Bits

Sweet breads like brioche are often sliced too thick for this recipe. Be sure your bread is correctly sliced. You want a proper balance between bread and filling.

Other Bites

Replace the Asian pear with strawberry slices and sprinkle grated semisweet chocolate over the cream cheese before sandwiching together. Then use grated chocolate for the decorative edge.

Banana Morsels

This sweet open sandwich is great way to use up overripe bananas. Their ripeness only adds to the flavor.

Yield: 32 sandwiches

1 loaf banana bread, cut to measure 4 x 8 x 4 inches

Apricot jelly

¼ cup heavy cream, whipped

1 to 2 bananas, ripe but firm

Round cutter measuring 1½ inch

Cut the loaf into sixteen ½-inch slices and cut out 2 round shapes from each.

Heat the apricot jelly in a small saucepan until the mixture is a slightly warmed, smooth liquid. Set aside.

Spread each round with a thin layer of whipped cream. Slice bananas thinly and arrange slices decoratively on top of the cream. Using a pastry brush, gently dab or brush the warmed jelly on top of the bananas. The jelly will make the bananas shiny and keep them from browning.

Serve immediately or store refrigerated, covered with plastic wrap, for up to several hours.

Little Bits

Quick breads can be crumbly. To get clean and even slices, chill or partially freeze the bread first. This will allow you to slice with precision.

Other Bites

For a unique twist, use brioche or any sweet bread and top the bread rounds with a thin coating of crème fraîche; garnish with lemon zest and wild blueberries.

Sandwich Stack, page 90.

Plated Sandwich Ideas

Now we get really creative. Using all of the shapes and fillings detailed in this book, get ready to turn your plate into a culinary work of art, impressing your guests with the kind of plating one rarely encounters outside of high-end restaurants.

- Sandwich Bouquet
- Dotted Roast Beef Sandwich Plate
- Stained Glass Sandwiches
- Sandwich Stacks

Sandwich Bouquet

Create a stylish "sandwich salad." It just takes a little planning. Almost any of the savory sandwiches in this book will do, but look for harmony and variety of flavors. Also be sure to incorporate at least three different colored breads. Lighter breads work best because they contrast well with the dark greens.

Bacon Chutney Tulips (page 32)

Cucumber Apricot Flowers (page 24)

Olive Spread Pinwheels (page 52)

Fresh basil, parsley, various greens, and scallions

Wash and dry all greens. Arrange them on an 8 to 10-inch plate in a bouquet pattern. Add sandwiches to represent flower blossoms. Slice scallions into pliable green strips and add underneath sandwiches to represent flower stalks. Use remaining herbs or greens as needed to represent leaves, filling any blank spaces on the plate.

Little Bits

Your sandwiches and greens can be prepared in advance. Just be sure to leave plenty of time for plating if you haven't made these bouquets before. Sometimes learning at the last minute can be difficult!

Pieces of tomato skin or colored peppers set into sandwich "blossoms" make perfect flower centers.

Other Bites

Most open-faced sandwiches can be used, though you may need to omit the garnish. Try to color-coordinate for an attractive ensemble.

Dotted Roast Beef Sandwich Plate

Think about those fancy desserts where the sauce is drawn or pooled on the plate. You can do the same with sandwiches. Use a single sandwich or a variety. Just learn a few condiment painting tricks and you can have stunning presentations every time.

Yield: 4 plated servings

24 small roast beef sandwiches on white, rye, and dark bread, cut into triangles

Mustard

Mayonnaise

Parsley or alfalfa sprouts, as garnish

Plastic squeeze bottles with narrow tips

Wooden skewer

First, choose a plate that will enhance your sandwich design and provide a clean canvas for painting on; a solid colored plate or one with a minimal pattern works well.

Fill 2 plastic squeeze bottles with mustard and mayonnaise, respectively. Place 6 triangle sandwiches in a circle pointing toward the center of the plate. Carefully squeeze out 3 circles of mayonnaise measuring 1, ¾ and ½ inches between each sandwich. With the mustard bottle, squeeze out smaller dots of mustard on top of the mayonnaise dots to measure ½ inch, ¼ inch and ⅛ inch, respectively.

Garnish the plate with a few pieces of parsley or sprouts and serve.

Plates can be made up in advance and covered with plastic wrap for 3 to 4 hours.

Little Bits

Use a dinner-size plate; otherwise you may not have enough space for decorating.

Other Bites

Make your garnished sandwich plates even fancier. Using a wooden skewer, place the point in the center of the ½-inch mustard dot and drag the toothpick straight down through all three dots. The slight drag will turn your dots into hearts!

For a simpler alternative, use glazed ham slices in place of sandwiches and use honey, mustard, and mayonnaise for painting.

Stained Glass Sandwiches

Simple, yet impressive. Serve to a crowd for maximum "wows."

Choose three or four same-shaped sandwiches
made with different breads. Triangles, squares,
and rectangles are easiest to work with.

Garnish options:

Parsley

Curled scallions

Thyme sprigs

Nuts

Dried fruits

Prepare the sandwiches. Place corners together in a circular formation for a star pattern. For other arrangements, consult a quilting pattern book. Herbs stuck into the corners make a nice finishing touch.

Little Bits

Plan ahead. Carefully count the number of sandwiches, condiments, and garnishes you will need per serving to make sure you have enough for each plate.

Other Bites

You can also use shapes that don't fit neatly together. Think outside the box!

Sandwich Stacks

If stacked entrees in restaurants are all the rage, why can't we do it at home? With the sandwiches in this book, it's easy.

Yield: 6 stacks

Smoked Turkey and Dried Fruit Pâté Squares filling (page 14)

12 slices firm white bread

Curry Cashew Bites filling, ½ recipe (page 18)

4 slices firm whole wheat bread

English Style Potted Ham Shapes filling, ½ recipe (page 44)

2 slices firm white bread

Dried cranberries, almonds, cashews, small gherkins, parsley, and/or thyme sprigs, as garnish

Square cutter measuring 1 inch

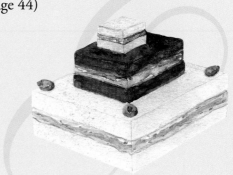

Cut the 12 slices of white bread into 3 x 3-inch squares. Make 6 smoked turkey sandwiches.

Using the whole wheat slices, prepare 2 curry cashew sandwiches. Cut off the crusts and cut each into 4 equal square sandwiches (you will need only 6 for this recipe).

Using the 2 slices of white bread, make a sandwich with the potted ham filling. Remove the crusts and cut this sandwich into 6 equal squares. You will have filling left over that you can freeze or eat separately.

Arrange sandwiches into six 3-layered stacks. Sprinkle nuts, fruit, and herbs on and around sandwiches for garnish. Plant a sprig of parsley or thyme on top and serve.

Little Bits

You want your design to be the focus. Use plain or minimally decorated plates.

Other Bites

Serve the stack wrapped in rice, tissue, or parchment paper and neatly tied or folded closed. This is an attractive way to present any finger sandwich assortment.

Caper and Green Tea Squares, page 20.

Scoops

If you love sandwich fillings but can do without the bread, this chapter is for you. Serving fillings alone creates a whole new range of decorative and flavorful possibilities.

- Stuffed Tomato Cups
- Italian Shrimp and Beans
- Lentil Duck-Filled Grapes
- Danielle's Veggie Platter

Stuffed Tomato Cups

Dolmas without the fuss! This easy recipe takes grape leaves and their classic stuffing and puts them into halved tomatoes.

Yield: 6 tomato halves

3 tablespoons olive oil

1 medium white onion, finely chopped

4 scallions, finely chopped

12 grape leaves, stems snipped away and chopped into small pieces

1 cup long-grain rice

½ cup fresh fennel bulb, finely chopped

4 cloves garlic, finely minced

1 teaspoon cumin

Salt and fresh-ground black pepper

2 cups water

½ cup chopped dill

1 cup chopped flat leaf parsley

¼ cup fresh fennel fronds, finely chopped

4 tablespoons fresh mint, finely chopped

Juice of 1 lemon

3 large tomatoes

Extra dill or fennel fronds, as garnish

Heat 3 tablespoons of the oil in a large, heavy skillet, then add the onion and scallions. Cook over medium heat for 5 minutes until the onions are softened. Add the rice and cook for 5 minutes more. Stir in the fennel bulb, chopped grape leaves, garlic, cumin, ½ teaspoon salt, and water. Bring this to a boil and simmer for 10 minutes, until the water has been absorbed and the rice is cooked through. (You may need to add more water so the rice does not stick to the bottom of the pan.) Cool, and then stir in the herbs, lemon juice, salt, and pepper. Set aside.

Cut tomatoes in half with a sharp knife and scoop out the pulp to create cups. Equally divide the filling between the 6 tomato halves and garnish with dill or fennel fronds. Serve immediately or cover and chill until ready to serve.

Little Bits

Know your audience: some don't like tomatoes, others don't eat fennel, and some won't like the mint!

Other Bites

Use an herbed cheese spread. For a more sophisticated flavor combination, replace the watercress with arugula and the apple with crispy onion rings.

Italian Shrimp and Beans

You might think shrimp and beans would not go well together, but the result may surprise you!

Yield: 4 cups

2-15 ounce cans white beans, with liquid

3 large cloves garlic, crushed

2 bay leaves

⅓ cup chopped fresh parsley

2 tablespoons tarragon white wine vinegar

2 tablespoon olive oil

¼ teaspoon salt

½ pound small shrimp, peeled and cooked

¾ cup diced red bell pepper

⅛ teaspoon ground red pepper

2 medium cloves garlic, pressed

½ cup finely chopped celery

3-inch celery stalks with leaves, as garnish

Extra parsley, as garnish

Combine the beans, their liquid, garlic, and bay leaves in a medium saucepan. Simmer at low heat for 40 minutes. Drain beans, reserving the liquid and discarding the bay leaves.

Return the liquid to the saucepan and boil until reduced to about ½ cup.

Combine the liquid, beans, parsley, 2 tablespoons vinegar, olive oil, and salt in a large bowl; toss and set aside.

Add the shrimp, bell pepper, remaining vinegar, red pepper, and pressed garlic to the beans mixture; stir in chopped celery.

Decoratively arrange celery stalks fanning out from the center of the plate. Mound the bean and shrimp mixture in the center and garnish with parsley.

Little Bits

Convert the shrimp and beans to a sandwich filling by mashing the beans and chopping the shrimp before mixing.

Other Bites

Serve filling atop broad, thin slices of jicama.

Lentil Duck-Filled Grapes

I love duck, especially in this unique combination. Try it and I'll wager one of my favorites will soon be yours too.

Yield: 24 filled grapes

1 cup dried lentils

1 large clove garlic, finely chopped

2½ teaspoons salt

½ cup seeded, diced tomatoes

4 large scallions, finely chopped

¼ cup fresh basil, finely chopped

About 50 large globe grapes, ½ cup of them chopped

1 tablespoon red wine vinegar

2 tablespoons extra virgin oil

¼ teaspoon black pepper

1 duck breast, roasted, chopped small

Melon baller

In a 2-quart saucepan, bring lentils, garlic, ½ teaspoon salt, and 4 cups of water to a boil. Reduce heat and simmer, uncovered, about 30 minutes or until lentils are just tender. Drain and put in a medium-sized bowl. Let cool to room temperature.

Toss lentils with tomatoes, scallions, basil, grapes, vinegar, oil, pepper, duck, and the other ½ teaspoon salt.

Using a small sharp paring knife, cut a ¼ inch off both ends of each grape. Then carefully carve out a hole out of one end with the melon baller. Fill with duck lentil filling, stand grapes up on a plate, and serve at room temperature.

———— ⟲ ————

Little Bits

Grape containers can be prepared a day in advance; just keep them in a chilled, covered container until ready to use.

Other Bites

Try stuffing Lady apples, Forelle pears, kumquats, or large strawberries; they all complement savory fillings.

Danielle's Veggie Platter

My sister is a strict vegetarian and spends a lot of time finding and testing great tasting meatless dishes. This is one of her favorites. Even those who don't care for tofu often enjoy this recipe.

Yield: 2 cups

1 pound tofu (semi-firm)

¼ cup mayonnaise

1 whole green onion, chopped

1 tablespoon cilantro, chopped

2 teaspoons soy sauce or tamari

½ teaspoon curry powder

½ teaspoon chili powder

1 teaspoon brewers or nutritional yeast*

¼ teaspoon garlic power

1 cup finely diced green, red, yellow, and/or orange peppers

Small celery stalks with leaves, long thin sticks of blanched carrot, zucchini, yellow squash, French green beans, and/or stalks of broccoli (see Appendix)

Extra cilantro, finely chopped, as garnish

found in most health food stores

Drain the tofu in a strainer for 20 minutes by weighing the tofu down with a clean plastic bag filled with water. Discard the liquid. In a food processor, puree the tofu until smooth. Spoon the tofu into a medium-sized bowl and stir in all remaining ingredients except the blanched vegetables. Chill until ready to use.

Placed a mound of tofu in the center of a plate and decoratively arrange cilantro and vegetables around it.

Little Bits

Create a bowl out of a hollowed-out pepper or fold back the leaves of a small head of radicchio to create an open flower and spoon the mixture into the center.

Other Bites

Feta or cottage cheese (drained) mixed with chopped sun-dried tomatoes makes an easy, tasty pink spread.

From left: Apple Yogurt Happy Faces, page 106; Pineapple Cheese Flowers, page 104; Nutty Carrot Rounds, page 105.

Kid-Friendly Sandwiches

Adults and kids especially love finger food. And the same sandwich techniques will bring a smile to both.

- Pineapple Cheese Flowers
- Apple Yogurt Happy Faces
- Nutty Carrot Rounds

Pineapple Cheese Flowers

Healthy ingredients in a pretty package, these "edible flowers" are a child's gourmet treat.

Yield: 12 sandwiches

8 ounces whipped cream cheese

1 cup crushed pineapple, well drained

12 slices firm white bread

Extra crushed pineapple, as garnish

Flower-shaped cutter measuring 2½ inches

Round cutter measuring ¾ inch

In a small bowl using a rubber spatula, mix the cream cheese and pineapple until smooth.

Cut 2 flowers out of each slice of bread. Using the smaller circular cutter, cut a center hole out of half of the bread shapes. Spread the cheese and pineapple mix evenly over the 12 solid flowers and top with the cut out ones. Taking a small spoon, carefully fill the center with extra pineapple and serve.

Nutty Carrot Rounds

These sandwiches are so appetizing that kids will hardly know they are eating healthy ingredients. If open-faced sandwiches are too messy, this spread goes well between bread slices, too.

Yield: 24 sandwiches

1 package cream cheese (8 ounces), softened

1 cup shredded carrots

¾ cup shredded sharp cheddar cheese

½ cup toasted pecans, chopped

¼ cup raisins

¼ cup parsley, chopped

12 slices raisin bread or any kind of firm bread

Extra grated carrot, as garnish

24 pecan halves, as garnish

Round cutter measuring 1½ inches

Combine all ingredient, except bread and garnish, in a medium-sized bowl. Chill until ready to use. Cut 2 circles from each bread slice. Mound filling on top of each circle and sprinkle with extra grated carrot. Place a pecan half on top for garnish.

Apple Yogurt Happy Faces

These little faces bring back memories of my grandmother making faces with her spatula in breakfast pancakes to surprise me. Don't forget to start the yogurt straining the night before.

Yield: 16 sandwiches

2 cups yogurt

½ cup apple butter

1 to 2 large sweet apples

½ lemon

16 slices firm bread

Round cutter measuring 1½ inches

Pastry bag fitted with ½-inch round tip

Crescent moon aspic cutter measuring about ¾-inch

Place plain yogurt in a fine mesh sieve and set sieve over a bowl for 12 to 18 hours. Discard expelled liquid and store the remaining thickened yogurt in an airtight container until ready to use.

In a small bowl, mix the yogurt cheese and the apple butter. Set aside.

Cut 2 rounds from each slice of bread. Using the aspic cutter, cut 2 eyes and a mouth out of 16 of the slices. Using the round pastry tip cutter, cut out the noses.

With a sharp knife or mandolin, carefully slice, vertically, sixteen ¼-inch apple slices. With the round cutter, cut out a circle from each slice. Place these in a bowl and douse with lemon juice to prevent browning.

Spread the apple-yogurt mix evenly between the 16 solid rounds; top with apple slices and happy faces.

Tomato-Eyed Pyramids, page 58.

What to Do with Leftover Bread?

Waste is a sin in my kitchen, so when I started making fancy sandwiches, I had to find ways to use the scraps. The following recipes may help ease your conscience, too.

When bread pieces are clean (without filling attached), use for bread crumbs or croutons. When bread pieces have filling attached, keep adding them to a bag in the freezer until you have enough for one of the latter two recipes below. The filling will only add flavor to these two dishes.

- Bread Crumbs
- Croutons
- Savory Mushroom Bread Pudding
- Tomato Spinach Strata

Bread Crumbs

Dry bread pieces on a baking sheet placed in an oven overnight (the pilot light will be enough to dry them out by morning). When bread is dry and hard, grind in a food processor and store in an airtight container in the refrigerator or freezer.

Croutons

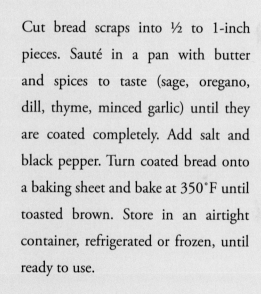

Cut bread scraps into ½ to 1-inch pieces. Sauté in a pan with butter and spices to taste (sage, oregano, dill, thyme, minced garlic) until they are coated completely. Add salt and black pepper. Turn coated bread onto a baking sheet and bake at 350°F until toasted brown. Store in an airtight container, refrigerated or frozen, until ready to use.

Savory Mushroom Bread Pudding

A wonderful side for a big meal or brunch, this dish is sure to please.

Yield: 12 servings

1 tablespoon butter

3 tablespoons olive oil

2 pounds assorted sliced mushrooms

4 teaspoons chopped garlic

1 tablespoon chopped fresh basil

1 tablespoon chopped fresh parsley

1 teaspoon dried sage

1 teaspoon dried thyme

5 large eggs

1 cup whipping cream

2 cups whole milk (do not use skim or low fat)

¼ cup freshly grated parmesan cheese

¾ teaspoon salt

½ teaspoon ground black pepper

6 cups 1-inch bread pieces

Preheat oven to 350°F. Lightly butter a 9 x 12-inch glass baking dish. Heat oil in a large, heavy frying pan over medium heat. Add mushrooms, garlic, and herbs, and sauté until mushrooms are brown and tender, about 15 minutes. Remove pan from heat. Season with salt and pepper.

Whisk remaining ingredients except bread in a large bowl to blend. Add bread and toss to coat. Let stand 15 minutes. Stir in herbed mushrooms and transfer to baking dish. Bake until pudding is brown, puffed up, and set in the center, about 1 hour. Serve warm.

Tomato Spinach Strata

A great brunch dish because you can make it in advance. This is a dish that serves a crowd and makes a dramatic appearance as well.

Yield: 10 servings

4 cups leftover bread pieces, toasted

1 tablespoon butter

1 cup chopped onion

4 garlic cloves, minced

8 ounces sliced mushrooms

1 package (10 ounces) frozen, chopped spinach, thawed and drained

½ teaspoon salt

½ teaspoon black pepper

4 thinly-sliced plum tomatoes (about 1 pound)

4 ounces feta cheese, crumbled

3 ounces Asiago cheese, grated (about ¾ cup)

3 cups whole milk

2 tablespoons Dijon mustard

1 tablespoons fresh oregano

5 large eggs, lightly beaten

4 large egg whites, lightly beaten

Preheat oven to 350°F. Lightly butter the surface of a 13 x 9-inch baking dish. Sprinkle half the toasted bread pieces over the bottom of the baking dish. Set aside.

In a heavy non-stick skillet over medium heat, sauté the onion, garlic, and mushrooms for about 5 minutes or until tender. Add the spinach, salt, and pepper. Spread this mixture evenly over the layer of bread.

Layer on the tomatoes, then sprinkle with feta and half the Asiago cheese. Arrange the remaining bread over the cheese.

Whisk the milk, mustard, oregano, eggs, and egg whites together in a medium-sized bowl. Pour onto the casserole and sprinkle remaining cheese on top. Cover and chill for 8 hours or overnight.

Bake uncovered for 35 to 40 minutes or until the top is lightly browned and center is set. Serve warm.

Cucumber Apricot Flowers, page 24.

Appendix

Toasting Nuts

Place any nut (except for pine nuts) on a baking sheet and place in an oven preheated to 350°F. Stir the nuts occasionally. Most nuts will take about 10 minutes to toast. You can usually tell when they're done from their aroma, but be careful: nuts can burn easily.

Pine nuts are especially delicate. Toast them in a frying pan over medium heat; you must stir the nuts frequently to prevent scorching.

Blanching Vegetables

Wash, drain, sort, trim, and cut vegetables to size.

Drop vegetables into a gallon of boiling water for the appropriate time (see below) and then remove. Do not mix vegetables that have different cooking times.

After removing vegetables from boiling water, immediately drop into ice water to stop cooking. Drain thoroughly before using.

Vegetable	Blanching Time (in minutes)
Asparagus, medium stalk	3
String or wax beans	3
Broccoli, 1½-inch flowerets	3
Carrots, sliced or in strips	2
Cauliflower, 1-inch flowerets	3
Celery sticks	3
Sweet peas in the pod	1½ to 2½
Pepper strips or rings	2

Resources

Atlantic Spice Company
North Truro, MA
800-316-7965
www.atlanticspice.com
Wide assortment of cooking spices.

The Baker's Catalog
Norwich, VT
800-827-6836
www.kingarthurflour.com
General cooking utensils, baking ingredients, and cookie cutters.

Bergen Supply Company
Pearl River, NY
845-735-4674
www.cookking.com
Professional-grade cooking utensils and equipment.

The Chef's Warehouse
www.ChefsWarehouse.com
Source for high end pastry ingredients and equipment.

Frontier Herbs
www.FrontierCoop.com
Great source for organic herbs.

J.B. Prince
New York, NY
212-683-3553
www.jbprince.com
Professional grade bakeware and equipment.

La Cuisine
Alexandria, VA
800-521-1176
www.lacuisineus.com
General equipment for cooking and baking and a wide assortment of cookie cutters.

New York Cake and Baking
Distributors
New York, NY
800-94-CAKE-9
www.nycake.com
General bakeware and cookie cutters.

Penzey's Spices
Muskego, WI
800-741-7787
www.penzeys.com
Great source for spices and herbs.

Sur la Table
Seattle, WA
800-243-0852
www.surlatable.com
Decorative baking equipment, cookie cutters, utensils, and more.

Sweet Celebrations
Edina, MN
800-328-6722
www.sweetc.com
Baking equipment, pastry tips, cookie cutters, and more.

Williams-Sonoma
San Francisco, CA
800-541-2233
www.williams-sonoma.com
Cooking equipment, cookie cutters, knives, and more.

Wilton Industries
Woodridge, IL
800-994-5866
www.wilton.com
Cookie cutters, pastry bags, tips, and assorted bakeware.

I do a fair amount of food-related charity work: it's both fun and rewarding. Standing in front of a local grocery store soliciting funds for the local food pantry one winter holiday, an attractive, well-dressed young woman asked to speak to me alone.

After stepping away from my table, she quietly told me that it was not long ago that she herself had benefited from the local food pantry. Only a few years before, her husband had left her and she had three small children to feed. She had a job at the time, but it didn't make her enough for both housing costs and food. If it hadn't been for the local pantry's support, she would not have gotten through those difficult years.

Happily, she told me that her life had turned around: she a had a new job, was in a new relationship, and her children were all well and happy. But she wanted to thank me for taking the time to stand in the cold to collect for this good cause.

I have never forgotten that exchange, so I know even just a meal or two in a time of need can make a big difference. That is why a portion of the proceeds of the sale of the Tastefully Small series will be given to America's Second Harvest Network, an umbrella organization supporting over 50,000 food charities in the U.S. For more information, visit www. secondharvest.org.

Index

A

alfalfa sprouts
Dotted Roast Beef Sandwich Plate 86

allspice 14

almonds 19
Sandwich Stacks 90
Smoked Turkey & Dried Fruit Pâté Squares 14

anise pods
Tea–Smoked Egg Diamonds 34

apples 99
Apple Yogurt Happy Faces 106
Beef, Apple & Watercress Spirals 38

apple butter 106

Apple Yogurt Happy Faces 102, 106

apricot preserves 68
Asian Pear Harvest Sandwiches 80
Banana Morsels 80
Grape, Brie and Walnut Cups 66
Peach Scallop Ceviche Tulips 68

apricots 14
Cucumber Apricot Flowers 24
Smoked Turkey & Dried Fruit Pâté Squares 14

arugula 24, 39, 95
Cucumber Apricot Flowers 24

Asiago cheese 114
Tomato Spinach Strata 114

Asian Pear Harvest Sandwiches 78

Austrian Cheese Triangles 40, 48

Avocado Pine Nut Layers 50

B

bacon
Bacon Chutney Tulips 32

bacon bits 71

Bacon Chutney Tulips 32, 84

baking powder
Lime Curd Boxes 74

balsamic vinegar 58
Grape, Brie and Walnut Cups 66
Tomato-Eyed Pyramids 58

banana bread
Banana Morsels 80

Banana Morsels 80

basil 84
    Cucumber Apricot Flowers 24
    Herbed Cheese Gift Boxes 56
    Lentil Duck-Filled Grapes 98
    Savory Mushroom Bread Pudding 112
    Tomato-Eyed Pyramids 58

bay leaves
    Italian Shrimp and Beans 96

bean sprouts
    Confetti Spread Butterflies 30

beef
    Jamaican Beef Turnovers 70

Beef, Apple and Watercress Spirals 36, 62

black pepper
    Austrian Cheese Triangles 40
    Avocado Pine Nut Layers 50
    Beef, Apple & Watercress Spirals 38
    Confetti Spread Butterflies 30
    Cucumber and Shrimp Triangles 16
    English Style Potted Ham Shapes 44
    Grape, Brie and Walnut Cups 66
    Grape, Brie, and Walnut Cups 66
    Herbed Cheese Gift Boxes 56
    Hummus Stacks 54
    Jamaican Beef Turnovers 70
    Lentil Duck-Filled Grapes 98
    Mock Crab Flowers 42
    Savory Mushroom Bread Pudding 112
    Stilton Pear Bites 46
    Stuffed Tomato Cups 94
    Tarragon Egg Boxes 60
    Tea–Smoked Egg Diamonds 34
    Tomato-Eyed Pyramids 58
    Tomato Spinach Strata 114

blueberries 15, 81

bread crumbs
    Jamaican Beef Turnovers 70

Bread Crumbs 110

bridal shower 30

Brie and Walnut Cups 66

brioche 81
    Asian Pear Harvest Sandwiches 78

broccoli
    Danielle's Veggie Platter 100

brown sugar
    Asian Pear Harvest Sandwiches 78

bruschetta 53, 58

butter 28, 111
    Austrian Cheese Triangles 40
    Cucumber and Shrimp Triangles 16
    English Style Potted Ham Shapes 44
    Fiesta Chicken Squares 28
    Grape, Brie, and Walnut Cups 66
    Jamaican Beef Turnovers 70
    Jam 'n Sponge Crosses 76
    Lime Curd Boxes 74
    Mock Crab Flowers 42
    Olive Spread Pinwheels 52
    Savory Mushroom Bread Pudding 112
    Smoked Salmon Hearts 26
    Tomato Spinach Strata 114

butter cream frosting 77

butterfly 30

butter molds 41

C

cake flour
    Lime Curd Boxes 74

Caper and Green Tea Squares 20, 92

capers 31
    Caper and Green Tea Squares 20

caraway seeds
    Austrian Cheese Triangles 40

carrot 57
    Danielle's Veggie Platter 100
    Nutty Carrot Rounds 105

cashews 18
    Avocado Pine Nut Layers 50
    Sandwich Stacks 90

caviar
    Confetti Spread Butterflies 30

Caviar-Tipped Rolls 36

cayenne pepper 19

celery
    Danielle's Veggie Platter 100
    Italian Shrimp and Beans 96

celery leaves 45

challah
    Bacon Chutney Tulips 32

cheddar cheese
    Bacon Chutney Tulips 32
    Mock Crab Flowers 42
    Nutty Carrot Rounds 105

cherries 15

chicken 17, 55, 71
    Fiesta Chicken Squares 28

chickpeas
    Hummus Stacks 54

chiffon cake 74
    Jam 'n Sponge Crosses 76

chili 71

chili powder
    Danielle's Veggie Platter 100

chives 35
    Austrian Cheese Triangles 40
    Grape, Brie and Walnut Cups 66

Herbed Cheese Gift Boxes 56

chocolate 79

chutney
    Bacon Chutney Tulips 32

cilantro
    Danielle's Veggie Platter 100
    Grape, Brie and Walnut Cups 66
    Peach Scallop Ceviche Tulips 68

cinnamon
    Asian Pear Harvest Sandwiches 78

cloves 45
    Tomato-Eyed Pyramids 58
    Tomato Spinach Strata 114

Confetti Spread Butterflies 12, 30

cookie cutters
    Apple Yogurt Happy Faces 106
    Bacon Chutney Tulips 32
    Banana Morsels 80
    Beef, Apple & Watercress Spirals 38
    Confetti Spread Butterflies 30
    Cucumber Apricot Flowers 24
    Fiesta Chicken Squares 28
    Grape, Brie and Walnut Cups 66, 68
    Grape, Brie, and Walnut Cups 66
    Mock Crab Flowers 42
    Nutty Carrot Rounds 105
    Peach Scallop Ceviche Tulips 68
    Pineapple Cheese Flowers 104
    Sandwich Stacks 90
    Smoked Salmon Hearts 26
    Tea-Smoked Egg Diamonds 34
    Tomato-Eyed Pyramids 58

coriander seed
    Avocado Pine Nut Layers 50

cornichons
    English Style Potted Ham Shapes 44

cottage cheese 101

cranberries
    Sandwich Stacks 90
    Smoked Turkey & Dried Fruit Pâté Squares 14

cream 80

cream cheese 14, 33
    Asian Pear Harvest Sandwiches 78
    Caper and Green Tea Squares 20
    Confetti Spread Butterflies 30
    Curry Cashew Bites 18
    Herbed Cheese Gift Boxes 56
    Nutty Carrot Rounds 105
    Olive Spread Pinwheels 52
    Pineapple Cheese Flowers 104
    Smoked Salmon Hearts 26

cream of tartar
    Lime Curd Boxes 74

crème fraîche 81
    Herbed Cheese Gift Boxes 56

Croutons 111

cucumber
    Cucumber and Shrimp Triangles 16
    Cucumber Apricot Flowers 24
    Grape, Brie and Walnut Cups 66
    Peach Scallop Ceviche Tulips 68

Cucumber and Shrimp Triangles 12, 16

Cucumber Apricot Flowers 24, 84, 116

Cucumber Apricot Sandwiches 48

cumin
    Fiesta Chicken Squares 28
    Stuffed Tomato Cups 94

curd cheese
    Austrian Cheese Triangles 40

curry
    Curry Cashew Bites 18
    Danielle's Veggie Platter 100
    Jamaican Beef Turnovers 70

Curry Cashew Bites 18, 90

D

Danielle's Veggie Platter 100

dark bread
    Austrian Cheese Triangles 40
    Avocado Pine Nut Layers 50
    Confetti Spread Butterflies 30
    Herbed Cheese Gift Boxes 56

dijon mustard
    Austrian Cheese Triangles 40
    English Style Potted Ham Shapes 44
    Tea-Smoked Egg Diamonds 34
    Tomato Spinach Strata 114

dill 111
    Cucumber and Shrimp Triangles 16
    Mock Crab Flowers 42
    Smoked Salmon Hearts 26
    Stuffed Tomato Cups 94

dolmas 94

Dotted Roast Beef Sandwich Plate 86

duck
    Lentil Duck-Filled Grapes 98

E

egg bread
    Bacon Chutney Tulips 32

eggs
    Caviar-Tipped Rolls 64
    Lime Curd Boxes 74
    Mock Crab Flowers 42
    Savory Mushroom Bread Pudding 112
    Tarragon Egg Boxes 60
    Tea-Smoked Egg Diamonds 34

Tomato Spinach Strata 114

English Style Potted Ham Shapes 22, 44, 90

F

fennel
Stuffed Tomato Cups 94

feta cheese
Tomato Spinach Strata 114

Fiesta Chicken Squares 28, 36

figs
Smoked Turkey & Dried Fruit Pâté Squares 14

flour
Lime Curd Boxes 74

food processor 15, 21, 43, 45, 51, 55, 59, 65, 67, 110

fruit chutney
Bacon Chutney Tulips 32

fruit salad 67

G

garbanzo beans
Hummus Stacks 54

garlic 111
Avocado Pine Nut Layers 50
Grape, Brie and Walnut Cups 66
Herbed Cheese Gift Boxes 56
Hummus Stacks 54
Italian Shrimp and Beans 96
Jamaican Beef Turnovers 70
Lentil Duck-Filled Grapes 98
Savory Mushroom Bread Pudding 112
Stuffed Tomato Cups 94

garnish 17, 18

gherkins
English Style Potted Ham Shapes 44
Sandwich Stacks 90

granulated sugar
Lime Curd Boxes 74

grape leaves
Stuffed Tomato Cups 94

grapes 67
Grape, Brie and Walnut Cups 66
Lentil Duck-Filled Grapes 98

green beans
Danielle's Veggie Platter 100

green olives
Olive Spread Pinwheels 52

green pepper 28

greens 84

green tea leaves
Caper and Green Tea Squares 20

ground beef
Jamaican Beef Turnovers 70

guacamole 50

H

ham 44, 87
English Style Potted Ham Shapes 44

heavy cream 80

Herbed Cheese Gift Boxes 56

honey 67, 87
Smoked Turkey & Dried Fruit Pâté Squares 14

horizontally sliced bread 15

horseradish sauce
Beef, Apple & Watercress Spirals 38
English Style Potted Ham Shapes 44

Hummus Stacks 54

I

Italian Shrimp and Beans 96

J

jalapeño pepper 28, 45
    Jamaican Beef Turnovers 70

jam 51

Jamaican Beef Turnovers 22, 70

Jam 'n Sponge Crosses 72, 76

jicama 25, 97
    Grape, Brie and Walnut Cups 66
    Peach Scallop Ceviche Tulips 68

K

kosher salt
    Grape, Brie and Walnut Cups 66
    Tea-Smoked Egg Diamonds 34

kumquats 99

L

Lapsong Souchong tea
    Tea-Smoked Egg Diamonds 34

lemon
    Apple Yogurt Happy Faces 106
    Cucumber and Shrimp Triangles 16

lemon juice 16
    Asian Pear Harvest Sandwiches 78

Avocado Pine Nut Layers 50
Beef, Apple & Watercress Spirals 38
Hummus Stacks 54
Mock Crab Flowers 42
Olive Spread Pinwheels 52
Smoked Salmon Hearts 26
Stilton Pear Bites 46
Stuffed Tomato Cups 94
Tea-Smoked Egg Diamonds 34

lemon peel
    Tomato-Eyed Pyramids 58

lemon zest 81

lentils
    Lentil Duck-Filled Grapes 98

lettuce 95

Lime Curd Boxes 74

lime juice
    Avocado Pine Nut Layers 50
    Beef, Apple & Watercress Spirals 38
    Grape, Brie and Walnut Cups 66
    Lime Curd Boxes 74
    Peach Scallop Ceviche Tulips 68

lime zest 74

long-grain rice
    Stuffed Tomato Cups 94

M

made in advance
    Banana Morsels 80
    Caviar-Tipped Rolls 65
    Lentil Duck-Filled Grapes 98
    Sandwich Bouquet 84
    Tomato-Eyed Pyramids 59

marjoram
    Herbed Cheese Gift Boxes 56

marscapone
  Cucumber Apricot Flowers 24

marscapone cheese 24

mayonnaise
  Caviar-Tipped Rolls 64
  Danielle's Veggie Platter 100
  Dotted Roast Beef Sandwich Plate 86
  English Style Potted Ham Shapes 44
  Fiesta Chicken Squares 28
  Tea–Smoked Egg Diamonds 34

Melon baller
  Lentil Duck-Filled Grapes 98
  Lime Curd Boxes 74

milk
  Asian Pear Harvest Sandwiches 78
  Confetti Spread Butterflies 30
  Curry Cashew Bites 18
  Herbed Cheese Gift Boxes 56
  Savory Mushroom Bread Pudding 112
  Tarragon Egg Boxes 60
  Tomato Spinach Strata 114

Mint leaves
  Lime Curd Boxes 74
  Stuffed Tomato Cups 94

Mock Crab Flowers 36, 42

muffin pans
  Grape, Brie, and Walnut Cups 66
  Peach Scallop Ceviche Tulips 68

multigrain bread
  Hummus Stacks 54

mushrooms
  Savory Mushroom Bread Pudding 112
  Tomato Spinach Strata 114

mustard
  Austrian Cheese Triangles 40
  Dotted Roast Beef Sandwich Plate 86
  English Style Potted Ham Shapes 44

Tea–Smoked Egg Diamonds 34
Tomato Spinach Strata 114

N

Nutella 51

nutmeg 78
  Asian Pear Harvest Sandwiches 78

Nutty Carrot Rounds 102, 105

O

olive bread
  Tomato-Eyed Pyramids 58

olive oil
  Grape, Brie, and Walnut Cups 66
  Italian Shrimp and Beans 96
  Lentil Duck-Filled Grapes 98
  Savory Mushroom Bread Pudding 112
  Stuffed Tomato Cups 94

Olive Spread Pinwheels 48, 52, 84

onions 14
  Austrian Cheese Triangles 40
  Danielle's Veggie Platter 100
  Jamaican Beef Turnovers 70
  Stuffed Tomato Cups 94
  Tomato Spinach Strata 114

oregano 111
  Fiesta Chicken Squares 28
  Tomato Spinach Strata 114

P

paprika
  Austrian Cheese Triangles 40

parmesan cheese
  Savory Mushroom Bread Pudding 112

parsley 21, 55, 84
  Austrian Cheese Triangles 40
  Cucumber and Shrimp Triangles 16
  Dotted Roast Beef Sandwich Plate 86
  Herbed Cheese Gift Boxes 56
  Italian Shrimp and Beans 96
  Nutty Carrot Rounds 105
  Savory Mushroom Bread Pudding 112
  Stuffed Tomato Cups 94
  Tea-Smoked Egg Diamonds 34

pastry bag 43
  Apple Yogurt Happy Faces 106
  Austrian Cheese Triangles 40
  Confetti Spread Butterflies 30
  Tomato-Eyed Pyramids 58

pastry brush 69

peaches 15
  Grape, Brie and Walnut Cups 66
  Smoked Turkey & Dried Fruit Pâté Squares 14

Peach Scallop Ceviche Tulips 68

peanut butter
  Hummus Stacks 54

pear
  Asian Pear Harvest Sandwiches 78
  Stilton Pear Bites 46

pecans 66
  Grape, Brie and Walnut Cups 66
  Nutty Carrot Rounds 105

pepper 55
  green 28
  jalapeño 28, 45, 70
  orange 28
  red 58, 68, 96
  yellow 28

pimento 27
  Olive Spread Pinwheels 52

Pineapple Cheese Flowers 102, 104

pine nuts
  Avocado Pine Nut Layers 50

poppy seeds 65

prunes
  Bacon Chutney Tulips 32

pudding 75

pumpernickel bread
  Avocado Pine Nut Layers 50
  Smoked Turkey & Dried Fruit Pâté Squares 14
  Stilton Pear Bites 46
  Tea-Smoked Egg Diamonds 34

Q

quark
  Austrian Cheese Triangles 40

R

radicchio 95

raisin bread
  Nutty Carrot Rounds 105

raisins 75
  Nutty Carrot Rounds 105

rectangle 19

red pepper 96
  Peach Scallop Ceviche Tulips 68
  Tomato-Eyed Pyramids 58

red wine vinegar
  Lentil Duck-Filled Grapes 98

rice
  Stuffed Tomato Cups 94

roast beef
  Beef, Apple & Watercress Spirals 38

roast beef sandwiches 86

rosemary 19
  Grape, Brie, and Walnut Cups 66
  Olive Spread Pinwheels 52

rye bread
  English Style Potted Ham Shapes 44

S

sage 27, 111
  Savory Mushroom Bread Pudding 112

salmon
  Smoked Salmon Hearts 26

salsa 29

salt
  Avocado Pine Nut Layers 50
  Caviar-Tipped Rolls 64
  Cucumber Apricot Flowers 24
  Fiesta Chicken Squares 28
  Grape, Brie, and Walnut Cups 66
  Herbed Cheese Gift Boxes 56
  Hummus Stacks 54
  Italian Shrimp and Beans 96
  Jamaican Beef Turnovers 70
  Lime Curd Boxes 74
  Mock Crab Flowers 7, 36, 37, 42
  Savory Mushroom Bread Pudding 112
  Tarragon Egg Boxes 60
  Tea–Smoked Egg Diamonds 34
  Tomato-Eyed Pyramids 58
  Tomato Spinach Strata 114

Sandwich Bouquet 4, 84

Sandwich Stack 82

sauce, horseradish 38

Savory Mushroom Bread Pudding 112

scallions 84
  Avocado Pine Nut Layers 50
  Grape, Brie and Walnut Cups 66
  Grape, Brie, and Walnut Cups 66
  Jamaican Beef Turnovers 70
  Lentil Duck-Filled Grapes 98
  Stuffed Tomato Cups 94
  Tarragon Egg Boxes 60

scallops
  Grape, Brie and Walnut Cups 66
  Peach Scallop Ceviche Tulips 68

shallots
  Caper and Green Tea Squares 20
  Fiesta Chicken Squares 28
  Olive Spread Pinwheels 52
  Smoked Salmon Hearts 26

sherry
  English Style Potted Ham Shapes 44

shrimp
  Cucumber and Shrimp Triangles 16
  Italian Shrimp and Beans 96

Smoked Salmon Hearts 22, 26

Smoked Turkey & Dried Fruit Pâté Squares 14, 90

sour cream
  Caviar-Tipped Rolls 64
  Smoked Turkey & Dried Fruit Pâté Squares 14

soy sauce
  Danielle's Veggie Platter 100
  Tea–Smoked Egg Diamonds 34

spinach
  Tomato Spinach Strata 114

squash
  Danielle's Veggie Platter 100

Stained Glass Sandwiches 88

Stilton Pear Bites 36, 46

strawberries 67, 79, 99

strawberry jam
  Jam 'n Sponge Crosses 76

Stuffed Tomato Cups 94

sugar
  Lime Curd Boxes 74

T

Tabasco sauce
  Avocado Pine Nut Layers 50
  Mock Crab Flowers 42

tamari
  Danielle's Veggie Platter 100

tarragon
  Herbed Cheese Gift Boxes 56
  Smoked Salmon Hearts 26
  Tarragon Egg Boxes 60

Tarragon Egg Boxes 22, 60

Tea-Smoked Egg Diamonds 34

thyme 45, 47, 111
  Jamaican Beef Turnovers 70
  Olive Spread Pinwheels 52
  Sandwich Stacks 90
  Savory Mushroom Bread Pudding 112

toasting 21, 45, 61, 69, 71, 75, 111

tofu
  Danielle's Veggie Platter 100

tomato 21, 85
  Avocado Pine Nut Layers 50
  Confetti Spread Butterflies 30
  Fiesta Chicken Squares 28
  Lentil Duck-Filled Grapes 98
  Mock Crab Flowers 42
  Stuffed Tomato Cups 94

Tomato-Eyed Pyramids 58
Tomato Spinach Strata 114

Tomato-Eyed Pyramids 58, 108

Tomato Spinach Strata 114

triangle 17

tuna 17, 31

turkey 55

U

Unsalted butter 42
  English Style Potted Ham Shapes 44
  Grape, Brie and Walnut Cups 66
  Lime Curd Boxes 74
  Mock Crab Flowers 42
  Olive Spread Pinwheels 52
  Tarragon Egg Boxes 60

V

vanilla extract 74
  Asian Pear Harvest Sandwiches 78
  Lime Curd Boxes 74

vegetable oil 42
  Grape, Brie and Walnut Cups 66
  Lime Curd Boxes 74
  Mock Crab Flowers 42
  Peach Scallop Ceviche Tulips 68
  Tarragon Egg Boxes 60

vinegar 98
  Grape, Brie and Walnut Cups 66
  Italian Shrimp and Beans 96
  Lentil Duck-Filled Grapes 98
  Tomato-Eyed Pyramids 58

W

walnuts 19
  Asian Pear Harvest Sandwiches 78
  Avocado Pine Nut Layers 50
  Tomato-Eyed Pyramids 58

water
  Lime Curd Boxes 74
  Stuffed Tomato Cups 94

water chestnuts 25

watercress 95
  Beef, Apple & Watercress Spirals 38
  Olive Spread Pinwheels 52
  Stilton Pear Bites 46

wheat bread 14
  Savory Mushroom Bread Pudding 112
  Smoked Turkey & Dried Fruit Pâté Squares 14

whipping cream
  Savory Mushroom Bread Pudding 112

white beans
  Italian Shrimp and Beans 96

white bread 16
  Apple Yogurt Happy Faces 106
  Avocado Pine Nut Layers 50
  Caper and Green Tea Squares 20
  Caviar-Tipped Rolls 64
  Cucumber and Shrimp Triangles 16
  Cucumber Apricot Flowers 24
  Fiesta Chicken Squares 28
  Grape, Brie, and Walnut Cups 66
  Hummus Stacks 54
  Jamaican Beef Turnovers 70
  Mock Crab Flowers 42
  Peach Scallop Ceviche Tulips 68
  Pineapple Cheese Flowers 104
  Sandwich Stacks 90
  Savory Mushroom Bread Pudding 112
  Smoked Salmon Hearts 26
  Tarragon Egg Boxes 60

white pepper
  Caviar-Tipped Rolls 64

white wine vinegar
  Italian Shrimp and Beans 96

whole grain bread
  Beef, Apple & Watercress Spirals 38

whole wheat bread
  Caper and Green Tea Squares 20
  Cucumber Apricot Flowers 24
  Curry Cashew Bites 18
  Fiesta Chicken Squares 28
  Grape, Brie and Walnut Cups 66
  Herbed Cheese Gift Boxes 56
  Olive Spread Pinwheels 52
  Peach Scallop Ceviche Tulips 68
  Sandwich Stacks 90
  Savory Mushroom Bread Pudding 112

Worcestershire sauce
  Avocado Pine Nut Layers 50

Y

yeast
  Danielle's Veggie Platter 100

yogurt
  Apple Yogurt Happy Faces 106
  Beef, Apple & Watercress Spirals 38
  Cucumber and Shrimp Triangles 16
  Herbed Cheese Gift Boxes 56

Z

zucchini
  Confetti Spread Butterflies 30
  Danielle's Veggie Platter 100